Microwave Cooking ·
101 Unique Uses

from Litton

Litton Microwave Cooking Products, Minneapolis, Minnesota

CERTIFIED FOR
MICROWAVE COOKING

LITTON
Microwave
Cooking
Products

CREDITS:

Design & Production: Cy DeCosse Creative Department, Inc.
Author: Barbara Methven
Art Director: Jan Huibregtse
Production Coordinators: Elizabeth Woods, Mary Ann Knox, Christine Watkins, Bonita Machel
Photographers: Buck Holzemer, Steve McHugh, Graham Brown, Jill Greer
Food Stylists: Lynn Lohmann, Susan Zechmann
Home Economists: Peggy Lamb, Kathy Weber
Typesetting: Jennie Smith
Color Separations: Weston Engraving Co., Inc.
Printing: Moebius Printing Co.

This is no ordinary recipe book. It's like a cooking school in your home, ready to answer questions on the spot. Step-by-step photographs show you how to prepare food for microwaving, what to do during cooking, how to tell when the food is done. A new photo technique shows you how foods look during microwaving.

The foods selected for this book are basic in several ways. All microwave well and demonstrate the advantages of microwaving. They are popular foods you prepare frequently, so the book will be useful in day-to-day cooking. Each food illustrates a principle or technique of microwaving which you can apply to similar recipes you find in magazines or other cookbooks.

This book was designed to obtain good results in all brands of ovens. Techniques may vary from the cookbook developed for your oven. If rotating foods is unnecessary in your oven, that technique may be eliminated. All foods are cooked at either High or 50% power (Medium). The Defrost setting on earlier ovens and Simmer setting on current ovens may be used when Medium is called for. This simplifies the choice of settings while you become familiar with the reasons why different foods require different power levels.

Microwaving is easy as well as fast. The skills you develop with this book will help you make full and confident use of your microwave oven.

The Litton Microwave
Cooking Center

Contents

What You Need to Know Before You Start

This is not an ordinary recipe book; it's an idea book. It gives you directions for microwave secrets to make food preparation easier. The simple recipes included in this book illustrate techniques or show you how to use the good ideas.

You already know how the microwave oven saves time; this book suggests new ways for even greater time savings. It also helps you save money.

Make homemade baby food that costs less than ready-prepared. Use the microwave to soften brown sugar and honey or to refresh stale snacks. Use lemon and orange peels to make candied or dried peel and flavored extracts.

How to Use This Book

Unlike most recipe books, this book is not arranged according to food categories from appetizers to desserts. Following is a brief description of how each section creatively uses the microwave.

Adapting Recipes for the Microwave

This section provides guidelines to tailor the size of microwave recipes to suit your needs or adapt conventional recipes for microwave use.

Using Your Microwave With Other Appliances

Get full use from your microwave oven by using it in combination with other appliances to achieve new results. Team the microwave with your conventional oven, range top, barbecue grill, deep-fat fryer, toaster and food processor.

Softening & Melting

The microwave oven softens or melts foods with superlative ease. This section features butter, cheese and chocolate, but it also includes a variety of other foods, from ice cream to tortillas.

Special Effects

For the cook with more taste than time, this section provides microwave shortcuts to classic dishes, plus some dramatic effects you can achieve only with microwave. Browning secrets for meat and baked goods add eye and appetite appeal. One-dish cooking offers main dishes and desserts for single servings or a full recipe.

Fruits, Peels & Nuts

The microwave oven brings ease and speed to the preparation of fruits, peels and nuts. Use them for cooking and snacking, as well as for flavoring or garnishing other foods.

Homemade Specialties

Microwave small batches of jelly and fruit syrups for variety and freshly made flavor year-round. Brighten your menus with money-saving pickles, flavored vinegars, and easy homemade liqueurs.

Just for Fun

Add to your range of quick microwave snacks. The section for children provides treats kids can fix for themselves, plus foods a parent can microwave for them. For amusement, try the useful and decorative craft of microwaving baker's clay.

General Microwave Tips

This assortment of food and household tips saves work, time and money. For example, learn how to make your own sweetened condensed milk, yogurt, liquid soap, and lip gloss.

Microwave Terms You Need to Know

The microwave oven does more than cook. It performs some steps in food preparation which no conventional appliance can do, and speeds up others which take more time conventionally.

Soften. Microwave the food, such as butter, cream cheese or ice cream, until it is of spreadable consistency but still holds its shape.

Melt. Microwave solid food until it changes to a liquid state or loses its original shape. Butter becomes pourable. Cheese loses its shape and spreads. Chocolate holds its shape until stirred.

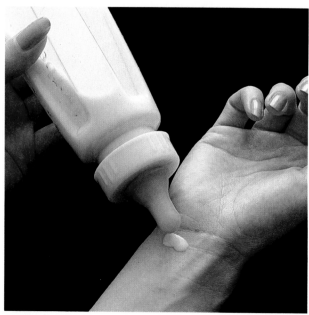

Warm. Microwave the food to remove the chill or raise the temperature slightly (105° to 114°F.). Solids should feel warm to the touch. A few drops of liquid on inner wrist will feel slightly above body temperature.

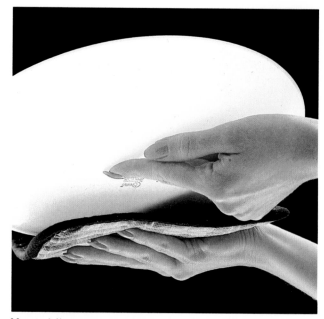

Heat. Microwave the food until it reaches serving temperature (140° to 160°F.). When food is hot, liquid steams and the bottom of the dish feels warm to the touch.

Keeping Food Hot

When serving food in its cooking dish, you may notice that food cooked in the microwave cools more quickly than food cooked conventionally. Here's why. In conventional cooking the pan becomes hot, then transfers heat to the food. In microwave cooking, the opposite is true. Microwave energy heats the food first, then transfers heat to the dish. After short microwave cooking times, the dish may remain cool. As the food stands after cooking, heat from the food transfers to the dish, causing the food to cool more quickly.

After short cooking times, microwave dishes do not become as hot as dishes used in conventional cooking. You may not need pot holders to handle microwave cooking dishes. However, longer cooking times do cause dishes to become hot, so care should be taken when handling and serving.

Insulating the dish by placing it in a basket or quilted casserole carrier will keep it warm and make it look attractive. Or, tie colorful cloth napkins around the dish.

Covering the dish during cooking and standing time helps retain heat. Casserole lids and plastic wrap hold in steam. Wax paper holds in heat without holding in steam.

Cooking and serving in the same dish will help food stay hot if the cooking time is long enough to heat the dish as well as the food. Choose dishes which hold heat well.

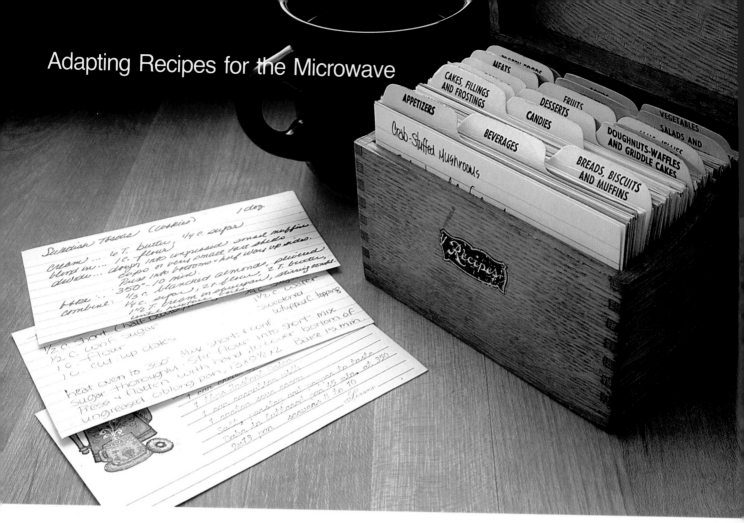

Adapting Recipes for the Microwave

Once you become familiar with microwave cooking, you can make changes in microwave recipes to suit your needs, or adapt many of your favorite conventional recipes for preparation in the microwave oven.

You may want to increase or decrease the yield of a microwave recipe to make it fit your family size or the number of guests you are serving. In microwave cooking, a change in the amount of food cooked usually requires a change in time.

Favorite recipes can be converted for low-calorie or low-salt diets and still be good-tasting. Fat is not required to prevent sticking in microwave cooking, even when you cook lean foods like fish fillets or skinned chicken. Special diet recipes which call for a non-stick frying pan or spray coating adapt well. Microwaving brings out the natural flavor of foods like fresh vegetables, so you can cook without salt; season lightly with herbs and spices.

Whether you want to convert a conventional recipe or adapt a microwave recipe to your needs, the guidelines in this section will point out most of the changes you need to make.

Changing Yield of Microwave Recipes

Microwave time is affected by the amount of food cooked and the depth of food in the container. The same amount of food microwaves faster in a shallow container than it does in a deep one.

Choose a container which will keep the layer of food at the same depth as in the original recipe. The container should be deep enough to prevent boilover, and not so large that the food will be spread thinly on the bottom.

Halve a microwave recipe by using half the amount of all ingredients and microwaving for two-thirds the original time.

Double a microwave recipe by using twice the amount of solid ingredients and 1⅔ to 1¾ the amount of liquid. A doubled recipe will take one-half to two-thirds more time.

How to Change Regular Recipes to Microwave Recipes

Use the following four guidelines to convert many conventional recipes to microwave, with minor changes to suit microwave cooking techniques and speed.

Step 1: Choose Recipe

Choose recipes which make no more than six to eight servings. Since more food takes more time, you will lose the advantage of microwave speed if you convert larger quantities. Look for conventional recipes which have one or more of the following features.

Cooking techniques similar to those used in microwaving, such as stirring, steaming or covering, indicate that the recipe will adapt well to microwaving.

Moist ingredients, such as poultry pieces, ground meat, vegetables, fruits, or sauces microwave well and are easy to adapt.

Rich foods, like quick-cooking candies, bar cookies, or layer cakes can be adapted.

(continued on next page)

Step 2: Adjust Ingredients & Methods

Foods which are warmed or heated, such as dips, spreads, or casseroles made with precooked ingredients, can be adapted for microwaving without a change in ingredients or preparation for cooking. Other foods may require special microwaving techniques. Check microwave recipes for the type of food you wish to prepare. You'll notice that pie shells are always microwaved before filling; cake dishes are always filled no more than half full; and quick bread loaves are elevated on a saucer to help the bottom cook evenly. Use the following guidelines to make changes in recipes.

Cut smaller pieces of meat and vegetables for stews and casseroles. Smaller, more uniform pieces microwave faster and more evenly.

Reduce liquid by one-third to one-half, then add more if needed for the consistency you want. Exceptions to this rule are recipes containing uncooked rice, pasta or dried beans and peas. These foods need the full amount of water to tenderize.

Reduce seasonings, such as salt. Microwaving enhances the natural flavor of food. Season the food to taste after microwaving is completed.

Add delicate ingredients, like cheese or shellfish, near the end of microwaving to prevent toughening and overcooking.

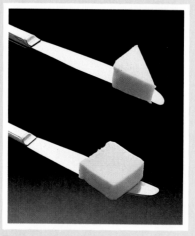

Reduce or omit fats in main dishes. Fats are not needed to prevent sticking. Use a small amount of butter or oil for flavor.

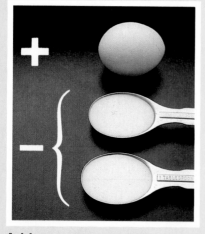

Add an extra egg and reduce liquid by 2 tablespoons to make tender cakes less fragile.

Step 3: Select Power Level

Compare your conventional recipe to a similar microwave recipe to determine the right power level. For example, cakes are microwaved first at 50% (Medium), then finished at High. A few minutes at High gets soups and stews started, then they microwave at 50% (Medium). The following factors influence the choice of power level used.

Type of liquid determines the power setting. Water, tomatoes, broth or wine can be microwaved at High. Delicate sauces containing cream, sour cream or cheese microwave at 50% (Medium) even when they are combined with ingredients normally microwaved at High.

Main ingredients like ground meats, poultry pieces or fish fillets microwave well at High. Pork chops and stew meat need time to tenderize and should be microwaved at 50% (Medium).

Stirring is important. If a casserole, such as lasagna, cannot be stirred during microwaving, reduce the power to 50% (Medium) and rotate the dish, even when all the ingredients are foods that microwave well at High.

Step 4: Estimate Time

The best guide to time is a microwave recipe which calls for similar amounts and types of main ingredients and liquid. If you can't find a similar recipe, try microwaving the food for one-fourth to one-half the conventional time. In either case, watch the food closely, adding more liquid if it is needed, and checking often for doneness.

Using Your Microwave With Other Appliances

Much of your cooking can be done with the microwave oven alone. However, you get even more benefit from your microwave when you use it as part of a total kitchen. Combine the convenience of your microwave with the effects you can achieve only with conventional appliances like the barbecue grill, deep-fat fryer, toaster, food processor or conventional oven.

Microwave & Conventional Oven

Team your microwave and conventional ovens to use each to maximum advantage. Microwave casseroles or potatoes for speed; finish them conventionally for a brown or crisp surface. Use your favorite recipes, but precook pie fillings or proof breads in the microwave, then bake conventionally. In any conventional recipe, look for steps you can do with the microwave to save time and clean-up, like scalding milk, melting chocolate or softening butter.

Breads & Rolls

Use the basic bread dough on the following page to make the following recipes:

Basic Rich Dough

1 pkg. active dry yeast
¼ cup warm water (110° to 115°F.)
½ cup milk
¼ cup shortening
1 egg, slightly beaten
2 tablespoons sugar
1 teaspoon salt
2½ to 3 cups all-purpose flour

How to Prepare Basic Rich Dough

Sprinkle yeast over warm water. Set aside. Place milk and shortening in large bowl. Microwave at High 1½ to 2 minutes, or until shortening is melted, stirring after each minute. Let cool to warm (115°F.).

Blend in yeast and remaining ingredients, except flour. Add flour, 1 cup at a time, beating at medium speed of electric mixer. Stir by hand when dough becomes stiff. Knead dough on a well-floured surface until smooth and elastic.

Place in lightly greased bowl. Cover with wax paper. Microwave at 10% (Low) 4 minutes. Let stand 15 minutes. Repeat microwaving and standing until dough is doubled in bulk. Punch down. Shape as directed in recipes on following pages.

How to Prepare Basic Rich Dough Loaf

Heat conventional oven to 400°F. Roll out dough on lightly floured board to 18 × 10-in. rectangle. Roll up from narrow end. Pinch ends. Place in greased 8 × 5-in. glass loaf dish.

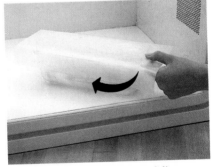

Cover with wax paper. Microwave at 10% (Low) 4 minutes. Let stand 15 minutes. Rotate dish. Repeat microwaving and standing until dough is doubled in bulk.

Bake about 25 minutes, or until loaf is golden brown and sounds hollow when tapped. Cool on wire rack.

15

Bagels

Basic Rich Dough, page 15
4 cups hot water
1 tablespoon sugar
1 egg white
1 tablespoon water
2 teaspoons sesame seed,
   optional

Makes 8 bagels

How to Prepare Bagels

Grease baking sheet; sprinkle with cornmeal to cover. Prepare and proof Basic Rich Dough as directed. Divide into eight equal pieces. Shape into balls. Cover; let rest 15 minutes.

Poke a hole all the way through center of each ball with index finger. Twirl around fingers to enlarge hole. Set aside.

Combine 4 cups hot water and the sugar in 3-qt. casserole. Cover with plastic wrap. Microwave at High 8 to 10 minutes, or until boiling.

Drop bagels into water. Microwave at High 2 minutes, rotating casserole after half the time. Poke center holes of bagels with handle of wooden spoon to prevent closing.

Turn bagels over. Microwave 1 to 2 minutes, or until firm to the touch. Meanwhile, heat conventional oven to 400°F. Drain bagels on paper towels.

Combine egg white and 1 tablespoon water; brush over bagels. Sprinkle with sesame seed. Place on prepared baking sheet. Bake 15 to 20 minutes, or until deep golden brown.

Caramel Rolls *Pictured on page 14*

Basic Rich Dough, page 15
5 tablespoons plus 1½ teaspoons butter or margarine, divided
⅓ cup granulated sugar
1½ teaspoons ground cinnamon

⅔ cup packed brown sugar
2 tablespoons light corn syrup
½ cup chopped pecans or walnuts, optional

Makes 9 rolls

Prepare and proof Basic Rich Dough as directed. Place on lightly floured board. Roll into 18 × 10-in. rectangle. Place 1 tablespoon plus 1½ teaspoons butter in custard cup or small bowl. Microwave at High 30 to 45 seconds, or until melted. Brush dough with melted butter to within ½ inch of edge.

In another small bowl combine granulated sugar and cinnamon. Sprinkle evenly over dough. Roll up tightly, starting with long side. Pinch edges to seal. Cut into nine 2-in. rolls. Place remaining 4 tablespoons butter in 9 × 9-in. baking dish. Microwave at High 45 to 60 seconds, or until melted. Stir in brown sugar and corn syrup.

Microwave at High 2 to 2½ minutes, or until boiling, stirring after each minute. Sprinkle with nuts. Arrange rolls, cut side up, in dish. Cover with wax paper. Microwave at 10% (Low) 4 minutes. Let stand 15 minutes. Rotate dish. Repeat microwaving and standing until dough is doubled in bulk. Meanwhile, heat conventional oven to 375°F. Remove wax paper from rolls. Bake 25 to 30 minutes, or until rolls are golden brown and sound hollow when tapped. Invert onto wire rack to cool.

Cinnamon Rolls

Basic Rich Dough, page 15
1 tablespoon plus 1½ teaspoons butter or margarine
⅓ cup granulated sugar
1½ teaspoons ground cinnamon

Glaze:
½ cup powdered sugar
1 tablespoon milk

Makes 9 rolls

Prepare and proof Basic Rich Dough as directed. Place on lightly floured board. Roll into 18 × 10-in. rectangle. Place butter in custard cup or small bowl. Microwave at High 30 to 45 seconds, or until melted. Brush dough with melted butter to within ½ inch of edge.

In another small bowl combine granulated sugar and cinnamon. Sprinkle evenly over dough. Roll up tightly, starting with long side. Pinch edges to seal. Cut into nine 2-in. rolls. Arrange rolls, cut side up, in greased 9 × 9-in. baking dish. Cover with wax paper.

Microwave at 10% (Low) 4 minutes. Let stand 15 minutes. Rotate dish. Repeat microwaving and standing until dough is doubled in bulk. Meanwhile, heat conventional oven to 375°F. Remove wax paper from rolls. Bake 25 to 35 minutes, or until rolls are golden brown and sound hollow when tapped. Remove from pan; cool on wire rack. In small bowl mix powdered sugar and milk until smooth. Drizzle over rolls.

Make-Ahead Dinner Rolls

To have homemade brown and serve rolls available at any time, microwave and freeze them ahead of time. To serve, defrost rolls quickly in the microwave, then brown them in a conventional oven.

Homemade Brown & Serve Dinner Rolls

Basic Rich Dough, page 15
1 tablespoon plus 1½ teaspoons butter or margarine

Makes 2 dozen rolls

Grease two 9-in. round baking dishes. Set aside. Prepare and proof Basic Rich Dough as directed. Divide in half. Cut each half into 12 equal pieces. Shape each piece into a ball. Arrange 12 balls in each dish. Cover with wax paper. Microwave one dish at a time at 10% (Low) 4 minutes. Let stand 15 minutes. Rotate dish. Repeat microwaving and standing until dough is doubled in bulk. Repeat with second dish.

Remove wax paper. Increase power to 50% (Medium). Microwave one dish at a time 2½ to 3 minutes, or until light and springy to the touch, rotating dish after each minute. Place butter in custard cup or small bowl. Microwave at High 30 to 45 seconds, or until melted. Brush rolls with half the butter. Remove rolls to wire rack to cool. Repeat with remaining dish. Wrap rolls in foil and freeze no longer than 1 month.

To defrost, microwave frozen rolls at High 1 to 1½ minutes, or until cool but not icy. Bake in preheated 400°F. conventional oven 10 to 15 minutes, or until deep golden brown.

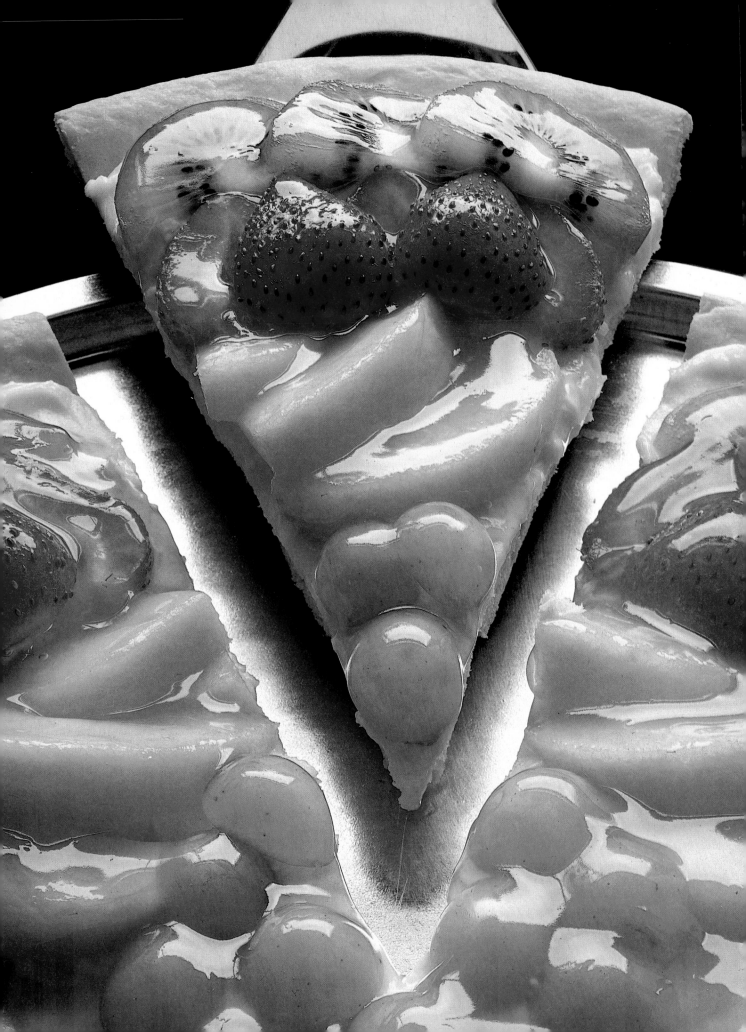

How to Prepare Pizza Crust From Basic Rich Dough

Prepare and proof Basic Rich Dough as directed, page 15. Divide dough in half. Heat conventional oven to 400°F.

Grease two 12-in. pizza pans. Lightly grease fingers; stretch dough gently to fit into pans.

Press dough around rim of pans to form standing edge. Generously prick crusts with lightly floured fork.

Bake on lowest rack 10 to 15 minutes, or until brown. Remove crusts to wire racks; cool completely before using.

Freeze crusts, if desired. Wrap in foil and freeze no longer than 1 month.

To defrost, remove foil. Place on microwave roasting rack. Microwave at High 1 minute. Let stand to complete defrosting.

◄ Fresh Fruit Pizza

1 Pizza Crust, above
1 pkg. (8 oz.) cream cheese, softened, page 44
¼ cup sugar
1 teaspoon grated fresh lemon peel
6 cups cut or sliced fresh fruit
⅔ cup apple juice
2 teaspoons arrowroot or cornstarch

Makes 12-in. pizza

Prepare and bake pizza crust as directed. Place softened cream cheese in medium bowl. Stir in sugar and lemon peel. Spread evenly over crust. Arrange fruit on crust. In 2-cup measure combine apple juice and arrowroot. Microwave at High 2 to 2½ minutes, or until clear and thickened, stirring after each minute. Cool until warm. Spoon over fruit. Refrigerate until glaze is set.

Pizza

1 Pizza Crust, above

Sauce:
1 can (8 oz.) whole tomatoes
1 can (8 oz.) tomato sauce
¼ cup chopped onion
1 teaspoon sugar
1 teaspoon olive oil

¼ teaspoon Italian seasoning
1 clove garlic, peeled and cut in half

Toppings:
Combination of cheese, meats, vegetables

Makes 12-in. pizza

Prepare and bake pizza crust as directed. Heat conventional oven to 375°F. In 1½-qt. casserole mix all sauce ingredients. Microwave at High 8 to 10 minutes, or until hot and bubbly and seasonings are well blended, stirring 2 or 3 times. Spread evenly over crust. Top with desired cheeses, meats or vegetables. For cooked meats, microwave as directed in chart, below, before adding to pizza. Bake pizza on middle rack of oven 10 to 15 minutes, or until cheese is melted and bubbly.

Meat	Microwave Time at High	Procedure
¼ lb. ground beef	1 - 3 min.	Stir to break apart after half the time. Drain.
¼ lb. ground pork sausage	3 - 5½ min.	

Crisp Microwaved Potatoes.
For drier and crisper skins on microwaved potatoes, combine microwave and conventional cooking. Preheat conventional oven to 375°F. Arrange pierced potatoes on roasting rack or in microwave-conventional muffin cups. Microwave at High as directed in the chart, below, turning over or rotating after half the time. Then bake potatoes in conventional oven for about 30 minutes, or until fork tender.

Amount	Microwave Time at High
1 potato	1½ - 2½ min.
2 potatoes	2½ - 3¼ min.
3 potatoes	3½ - 5 min.
4 potatoes	5¼ - 6¼ min.

Golden Brown Casseroles.
Microwave your favorite casserole as directed in the recipe. During the last 10 minutes of microwaving, preheat conventional oven to 400°F. Sprinkle casserole with crumb or cheese topping. Bake on middle rack of conventional oven for 10 to 15 minutes, or until top is golden brown.

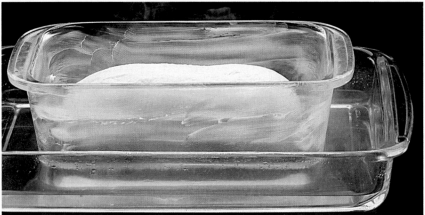

Defrost Frozen Convenience Bread Dough. Butter one frozen loaf on all sides and place in a greased 8×5-in. glass loaf dish. Measure 1 to 1½ cups water into 12×8-in. baking dish. Microwave at High until boiling. Place loaf dish in baking dish of hot water. Cover with wax paper. Reduce power to 50% (Medium). Microwave 2 minutes, rotating dish ¼ turn every minute. Turn dough over. Increase power to High. Microwave 2 minutes longer, rotating dish after 1 minute. Let stand 10 minutes. Dough should be defrosted and slightly warm. If not, continue to microwave 1 minute at a time until defrosted. Proof and bake conventionally as directed on the package.

Defrost Frozen Convenience Dinner Roll Dough. Place 12 dinner rolls in greased 10-in. glass pie plate. Cover with wax paper. Microwave at 50% (Medium) 2 to 3 minutes, or until warm to the touch, rotating after each minute and turning rolls over after half the time. Let stand 10 minutes. Proof and bake conventionally as directed on package.

Defrost Frozen Pot Pie. Remove pot pie from foil pan to 15- or 22-oz. individual casserole. Microwave at 50% (Medium) 3 to 6 minutes, or until wooden pick is easily inserted in center, rotating after half the time. Bake conventionally at temperature indicated on package 20 to 25 minutes, or until golden brown.

◀ **Frozen Homemade Two-Crust Pies.** During fruit season, prepare quantities of two-crust fruit pies. Freeze unbaked pies for later use. Defrost frozen pies in microwave, then bake in conventional oven for one-third to one-half the time.

Prepare pie: Microwave your favorite fruit filling ingredients at High 4 to 9 minutes, or until thickened, stirring every 2 minutes. The times are based on proportions for a 9-in. pie (4 to 6 cups fruit). Cool to room temperature. Prepare two-crust pastry as directed, page 23. Fit into 9-in. glass pie plate; spoon in fruit filling. Top with pastry, seal and flute. Do not bake. Wrap in foil and freeze no longer than 3 months.

To defrost pie: Heat conventional oven to temperature indicated in your recipe. Unwrap pie and microwave at 50% (Medium) 10 to 17 minutes, or until wooden pick can be easily inserted in center of pie, rotating after half the time. Bake in conventional oven as directed in recipe for one-third to one-half the suggested time. Shield crust edges with 3-in. strip of foil during last 10 minutes of baking to prevent edges from overbrowning.

Defrost Frozen Convenience Two-Crust Pies. To defrost frozen convenience two-crust pie, remove pie from metal pan to glass pie plate or 1½-qt. casserole cover. Microwave at 50% (Medium) 3½ to 6½ minutes per pound, rotating after half the time. Pie is defrosted when wooden pick can be easily inserted in center. Bake in preheated conventional oven as directed on package for one-third to one-half the recommended time. Shield crust edges with 3-in. strip of foil during last 10 minutes of baking to prevent edges from overbrowning.

Drop Cookie Dough. Prepare double batch of a drop cookie recipe. Bake one according to recipe; package second batch in freezer container. Freeze no longer than 1 month. To defrost, microwave dough in large bowl at 30% (Medium-Low) 6 to 8 minutes, turning over every 2 minutes; break apart. Let stand 5 to 10 minutes. Bake in conventional oven as directed in recipe.

Refrigerator Cookie Dough. Prepare double batch of your favorite refrigerator cookies. Bake one batch according to recipe and freeze the second for later use. Shape second batch into two 2-in. diameter logs. Wrap in wax paper; place in freezer bag. Freeze no longer than 1 month. To defrost, remove wrappings. Microwave at 30% (Medium-Low) 1 to 2 minutes, or until wooden pick can be easily inserted, but dough is still cool. Let stand 10 minutes. Slice and bake in conventional oven as directed in recipe.

Triple Layer Citrus Pie

One-Crust Pastry Shell, opposite

Lemon Layer:
½ cup sugar
2 tablespoons cornstarch
    Dash salt
¾ cup water
1 egg yolk
1 teaspoon fresh lemon peel
2 tablespoons fresh lemon juice
1 drop yellow food coloring

Lime Layer:
½ cup sugar
2 tablespoons cornstarch
    Dash salt
¾ cup water
1 egg yolk
1 teaspoon fresh lime peel
2 tablespoons fresh lime juice
1 drop green food coloring

Orange Layer:
½ cup sugar
2 tablespoons cornstarch
    Dash salt
¾ cup water
1 egg yolk
1 teaspoon fresh orange peel
2 tablespoons fresh orange juice
2 drops red food coloring and
    2 drops yellow food coloring

Meringue:
3 egg whites
¼ teaspoon cream of tartar
6 tablespoons sugar

Makes 9-in. pie

Prepare crust as directed; cool. Prepare lemon layer by combining sugar, cornstarch and salt in 4-cup measure or medium bowl. Slowly blend in water. Microwave at High 2½ to 3½ minutes, or until thickened and clear, stirring after half the time. Place egg yolk in custard cup or small bowl. Stir a small amount of hot mixture into egg

yolk. Return to hot mixture. Reduce power to 50% (Medium). Microwave 1 to 1½ minutes, or until thickened and set, stirring once during cooking. Stir in remaining lemon layer ingredients. Pour into cooled crust; spread to edges.

Repeat process with lime and orange layers.

Heat conventional oven to 375°F. Combine egg whites and cream of tartar in deep bowl. Beat at high speed of electric mixer until soft peaks form. Add sugar, 1 tablespoon at a time, continuing to beat until stiff peaks form. Spread over orange layer to edges of crust. Bake 8 to 12 minutes, or until brown. Cool before cutting.

One-Crust Pastry Shell

1 cup all-purpose flour
½ teaspoon salt
⅓ cup shortening
2 tablespoons butter or margarine, room temperature
3 tablespoons cold water

Makes 9-in. pie shell

Combine flour and salt in medium bowl; cut in shortening and butter, using pastry blender until particles resemble coarse crumbs or small peas. Sprinkle water over flour mixture while stirring with fork until particles are just moist enough to cling together and form a ball.

Flatten ball on floured board. Roll out to ⅛-in. thick circle, at least 2 inches larger than inverted pie plate. Fit into pie plate (use glass if microwaving). Trim pastry overhang to generous ½ inch; flute. Prick crust with fork continuously at bend and ½ inch apart on bottom and side.

Microwave at High 5 to 7 minutes, rotating dish ½ turn every 3 minutes. Check for doneness by looking through bottom of pie plate. Crust will not brown, but will appear dry and opaque when done. Or, bake in preheated 400°F. oven, 10 to 12 minutes, or until light golden brown. Cool before filling.

Variation:
Two-Crust Pastry: Double amounts of shortening, flour and salt; use 3 tablespoons butter or margarine and ⅓ to ½ cup cold water. Prepare as directed. Divide dough in half before rolling out. Fit bottom crust into 9-in. pie plate. Fill as desired. Add top crust; seal and flute. Cut slits in top crust and bake in conventional oven.

NOTE: To give microwave crust a conventional-baked appearance, see page 82.

Au Gratin Potatoes

2 lbs. baking potatoes, peeled and cut into ¾-in. cubes
1 medium onion, thinly sliced
¼ cup butter or margarine
¼ cup all-purpose flour
¾ teaspoon salt
⅛ teaspoon white pepper
1 cup milk
½ cup beer
2 cups shredded Cheddar cheese
Paprika

Serves 6

Heat conventional oven to 400°F. In 2-qt. casserole place cubed potatoes and onion slices; cover. Microwave at High 10 to 12 minutes, or until fork tender, stirring every 4 minutes. Cover and set aside. Place butter in 4-cup measure. Microwave at High 45 to 60 seconds, or until melted.

Add flour, salt and white pepper. Blend in milk and beer. Microwave at High 4 to 5 minutes, or until thickened, stirring after each minute. Stir in cheese until melted. Pour cheese sauce over cooked potatoes. Stir to coat. Sprinkle with paprika. Bake 10 to 15 minutes, or until light brown.

Microwave & Range Top

Most of the foods you might cook on the range top can be prepared faster and more easily in the microwave oven. A few, like crêpes and pancakes, can't be microwaved. Cook them conventionally and microwave their sauces or fillings. Combine the microwave and range top to save time. Cook pasta or rice conventionally while you microwave the sauce or main dish. Brown chops or steaks conventionally and complete cooking in the microwave.

Pasta & Sauce. Prepare sauces in the microwave oven while you cook pasta conventionally. Sauces made with tomatoes, broth, soup or milk are less sensitive to overheating and can be microwaved at High. Stirring occasionally keeps the sauce smooth and speeds cooking. When adding a meat which needs time to tenderize, microwave the sauce at 50% (Medium). Sauces made with cream or dairy sour cream should be microwaved at 50% (Medium) because they are sensitive to overheating. When cheese is added to a sauce, microwave at 50% (Medium) just until cheese melts.

Brown Pork Chops. Combine conventional browning with microwave speed. In 10-in. pyroceram skillet place about 2 tablespoons of vegetable oil. Add four 1-in. thick pork chops (8 to 9 oz. each). Fry over medium-high heat about 5 minutes on each side, or until brown; drain. Cover. Microwave at 50% (Medium) 11½ to 13 minutes, or until temperature in several places reaches 170°F., turning over and rearranging chops after half the time. Let stand, covered, 5 minutes.

Remove pork chops to serving platter. If desired, thicken drippings by blending in 1 tablespoon all-purpose flour for every ½ cup drippings. Microwave at High at 1-minute intervals, or until thickened, stirring after each minute. Serve with pork chops.

Crêpes

2 tablespoons butter or
    margarine
1¼ cups all-purpose flour
1½ cups milk
  1 egg
¼ teaspoon salt

              Makes 16 crêpes

Variation:
Whole Wheat Crêpes: Substitute ¼ cup whole wheat flour for ¼ cup all-purpose flour.

How to Prepare Crêpes

Microwave butter in small bowl at High 30 to 45 seconds, or until melted. Pour into blender container or medium bowl. Add remaining ingredients and blend until smooth. Refrigerate at least 1 hour.

Heat lightly oiled 6-in. skillet over medium heat on conventional range. Pour 2 tablespoons batter into skillet. Lift and swirl skillet to coat bottom. Cook 20 to 30 seconds, or until edges of crêpe are set.

Turn and brown other side. Set aside to cool. Repeat with remaining batter. Stack with wax paper between crêpes. Use in crêpe recipes, page 26, or freeze in quantities of eight for future use.

Wrap stacked crêpes in freezer storage bags; seal. Label and freeze no longer than 1 month.

To defrost, place stacked crêpes in oven. Microwave at 50% (Medium) 1½ to 2½ minutes, or until cool but not icy, rotating after half the time.

Let stand 5 minutes. Separate and use in Chicken Crêpes, page 26 or Strawberry Crêpes, page 27.

25

Chicken Crêpes

8 Crêpes, page 25
2 cups fresh broccoli flowerets
    or fresh asparagus cut into
    1-in. pieces
¼ cup water
1½ cups sliced fresh mushrooms
3 tablespoons finely chopped
    onion
2 tablespoons butter or
    margarine
2 tablespoons all-purpose
    flour
1 teaspoon instant chicken
    bouillon granules
¼ teaspoon salt
¼ teaspoon white pepper
⅛ teaspoon poultry seasoning
1½ cups milk
¾ cup shredded Monterey
    Jack or Swiss cheese
2 cups cut-up cooked
    chicken
2 tablespoons sliced almonds

Serves 4

Variation:
Ham Crêpes: Prepare as directed, below, substituting 2 cups shredded, fully cooked ham for the chicken. Omit the chicken bouillon granules in the sauce. Microwave as directed.

How to Prepare Chicken Crêpes

Prepare crêpes as directed. Set aside. Place broccoli flowerets or asparagus cuts in 2-qt. casserole. Add water; cover.

Microwave at High 4 to 6 minutes, or until tender-crisp, stirring after half the time. Drain. Add mushrooms; cover and set aside.

Combine onion and butter in 4-cup measure. Microwave at High 2 to 3 minutes, or until tender, stirring once. Stir in flour, bouillon granules, salt, pepper and poultry seasoning.

Strawberry Crêpes

8 Crêpes, page 25
2 pints fresh strawberries,
   hulled and sliced
1 tablespoon plus 1½
   teaspoons cornstarch
½ cup cold water
¼ cup plus 2 tablespoons
   granulated sugar
3 tablespoons orange liqueur
   or homemade Orange
   Liqueur, page 102
1 or 2 drops red food coloring,
   optional
   Powdered sugar, optional
   Prepared whipped topping
   or dairy sour cream

Serves 4

Prepare crêpes as directed. Set aside. Place ½ cup sliced strawberries in 4-cup measure or medium bowl. Set aside. Blend cornstarch into water. Add to ½ cup strawberries. Stir in granulated sugar and liqueur. Microwave at High 3½ to 4½ minutes, or until clear and thickened, stirring once. Stir in food coloring and remaining strawberries. Cool.

Place 2 tablespoons of filling on each crêpe; roll up. Sprinkle with powdered sugar, if desired. Top each crêpe with dollop of whipped topping.

Blend in milk. Microwave at High 3½ to 6 minutes, or until thickened and bubbly, stirring 2 times. Add cheese, stirring to melt. Reserve ⅓ cup sauce for topping crêpes.

Mix remaining sauce and the chicken into vegetables. Place about ½ cup filling in center of each crêpe. Roll up. Arrange in 12 × 8-in. glass baking dish.

Pour reserved sauce over crêpes. Sprinkle with almonds. Cover with wax paper. Microwave at 70% (Medium-High) 8 to 12 minutes, or until heated, rotating once. Let stand, covered, 5 minutes.

27

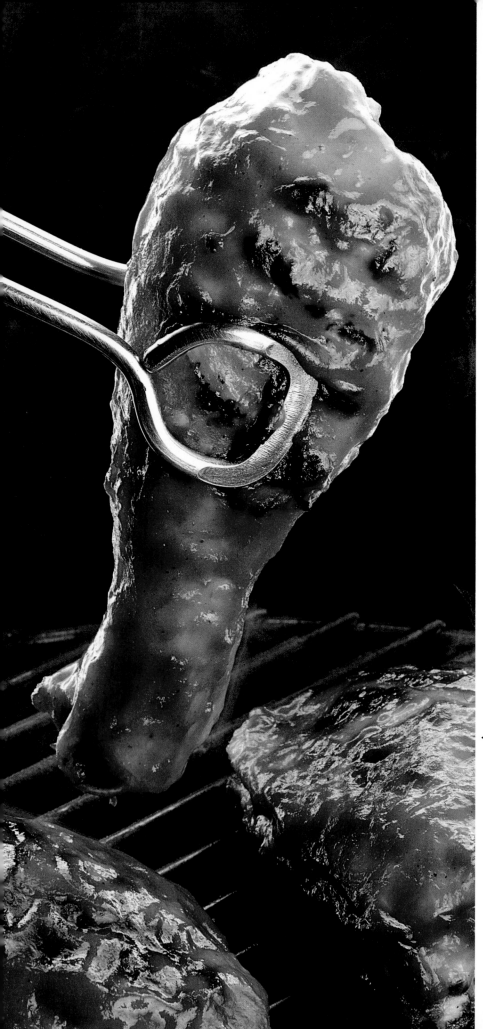

Microwave & Barbecue Grill

The barbecue grill produces a flavor that can't be duplicated by any other cooking method. When you combine the microwave with the grill, you get faster results with the same great barbecue taste.

Conventional barbecuing takes time, first to build a good bed of coals, and then to grill the meat slowly. If the fire is too hot, the food will be burned on the outside and raw in the center.

When you partially cook the meat in the microwave and then finish it on the grill, you save one-third to one-half the time. You can microwave the meat while the coals are heating. Best of all, your barbecue meat will be tender and juicy in a minimum of time.

◄ **Barbecued Chicken Pieces.** Cut 2½- to 3½-lb. broiler-fryer chicken into quarters or pieces. In 12 × 8-in. baking dish arrange chicken pieces with bony sides down and thick meaty portions to outside of dish. Cover with wax paper. Microwave at High 10 minutes, turning and rearranging pieces after half the time. Place on charcoal grill over hot coals. Baste with your favorite barbecue sauce. Grill 15 to 20 minutes, or until juices run clear. Serves 4.

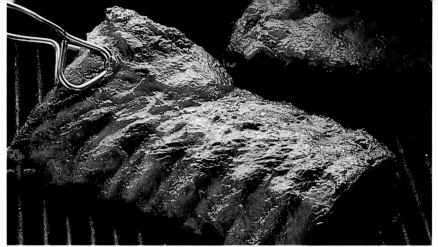

Barbecued Ribs. Arrange 3 to 4 pounds beef short ribs, pork spareribs, pork baby back ribs or pork country-style ribs in single layer in 12×8-in. baking dish or 3-qt. casserole. Overlap slightly as needed. Add ¼ cup water. Cover with plastic wrap. Microwave at High 5 minutes, rotating dish and rearranging pieces after half the time. Reduce power to 50% (Medium). Microwave 15 minutes, turning ribs over after half the time. Drain. Place on charcoal grill over hot coals. Baste with your favorite barbecue sauce. Grill about 20 to 25 minutes, or until fork tender. Serves 3 or 4.

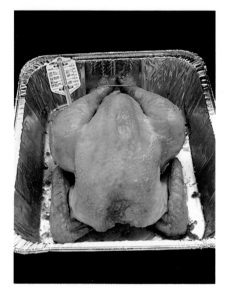

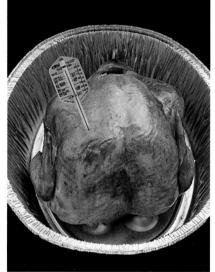

Grilled Whole Chicken. Fold wings under and tie legs of 2½- to 3½-lb. chicken. Place chicken, breast side down, in 12×8-in. baking dish. Microwave at High 3 minutes. Reduce power to 50% (Medium). Microwave 15 minutes, turning breast side up after half the time. Transfer to foil roasting pan. Place on charcoal grill over hot coals. Cover grill. Grill about 20 minutes, or until juices run clear and temperature in meaty portion of thigh reaches 185°F. Serves 4.

Grilled Whole Turkey. Place turkey, breast side up, in 12×8-in. glass baking dish. (Remove any metal clamps.) Microwave at High 10 minutes. Turn breast side down. Rotate dish ½ turn. Reduce power to 50% (Medium). Microwave 50 minutes, turning breast side up after 25 minutes. Transfer to foil roasting pan. Place on charcoal grill over very hot coals. Cover grill. Grill 30 to 40 minutes, or until juices run clear and temperature in meaty portion of thigh reaches 185°F. Serves 8 to 10.

Grilled Hamburgers & Hot Dogs. Freeze extra grilled hamburgers and hot dogs in foil no longer than 6 months. Microwave later for just-grilled taste. To defrost and heat, unwrap and place on plate. Microwave at 50% (Medium) as directed in chart, or until heated, turning after half the time.

Item	Microwave Time
1 hamburger	1¼ - 3 min.
2 hamburgers	2½ - 4 min.
1 hot dog	1 - 1½ min.
2 hot dogs	1½ - 2 min.

Microwave & Toaster

The microwave oven and the toaster complement each other. Freeze breads to extend storage time. Then use the microwave to defrost a whole loaf or one slice at a time. Toast bread to remove excess moisture and to crisp before you microwave sandwiches. Microwave frozen English muffins and bagels to defrost them so halves can be separated for toasting.

◄ Toastwiches

2 slices white, wheat or rye
  bread, toasted

Combination of the following:
Meat:
2 oz. sliced fully cooked turkey,
  beef, ham, or salami

Vegetables:
  Sliced tomatoes
  Fresh alfalfa sprouts
  Cucumber slices
  Onion slices
  Green onion
  Radish slices
  Green pepper slices

Cheese:
  Assorted cheese slices
  (Cheddar, American, Colby,
  Swiss, brick)

Condiments:
  Butter or margarine
  Mayonnaise or salad dressing
  Prepared mustard
  Catsup
  Dairy sour cream

Serves 1

Top one slice of toast with meat of your choice. Add vegetables as desired; top with a cheese slice. Place on paper towel-lined serving plate. Microwave at High 30 to 60 seconds, or until cheese melts. Spread remaining slice of toast with a condiment. Place on top of cheese to complete sandwich.

Quick Breakfast

Freeze extra homemade waffles and French toast. Heat them in the toaster while you warm maple or fruit syrup, page 107, in the microwave.

Defrost & Warm Frozen Bagels. Place one frozen bagel on napkin in oven. Microwave at High 15 to 30 seconds, or until warm; microwave two bagels at High 30 to 45 seconds. Separate and toast. Spread with softened cream cheese, page 44, if desired.

Defrost Bread

To defrost a 1½-lb. loaf of bakery bread, remove twist tie from bag. Place bread with wrapper in oven. Microwave at High 45 seconds to 1¼ minutes, or until bread is cool but not icy. Let stand 5 minutes to complete defrosting.

Mock Monte Cristo

2 slices frozen French toast, toasted
2 oz. thinly sliced fully cooked ham
1 slice (¾ oz.) Cheddar cheese
Prepared mustard
Dairy sour cream

Serves 1

Toast French toast as directed on package. Place ham, then cheese on one slice of French toast. Place on serving plate. Microwave at High 30 to 60 seconds, or until cheese melts. Spread remaining slice of French toast with mustard. Place on top of cheese to complete sandwich. Serve with dollop of sour cream.

Dessert Waffles

Apple Topping:
 1 can (20 oz.) apple pie filling
 2 tablespoons raisins
 ⅛ teaspoon ground nutmeg

Blueberry Topping:
 1 can (21 oz.) blueberry pie filling
 ½ teaspoon grated lemon peel or ¼ teaspoon Dried Lemon Peel, page 87
 ⅛ teaspoon ground allspice

Cherry Topping:
 1 can (21 oz.) cherry pie filling
 ¼ cup sliced almonds
 ¼ teaspoon almond extract

Waffles:
 4 frozen or homemade waffles, toasted
 1 pkg. (3 oz.) cream cheese, softened, page 44

Serves 4

Prepare desired topping by combining ingredients in medium bowl. Microwave at High 2½ to 4 minutes, or until heated, stirring after half the time. Set aside.

Toast waffles as directed on package. Spread each toasted waffle with one-fourth of the cream cheese. Top each with one-fourth of the fruit topping. Serve with dollop of whipped topping, if desired.

Microwave & Deep-Fat Fryer

The microwave oven teams up with the deep-fat fryer to produce delicious vegetables that are cooked tender and crisp but not greasy. For a make-ahead appetizer, prepare Deep-Fried Cheesy Vegetables, opposite, but do not deep-fry until just before serving. For non-greasy French fries, microwave a baking potato. Cut into quarters or eighths and deep-fry until light brown.

Reheat Deep-Fried Foods. Place deep-fried foods on serving plate. Microwave at 70% (Medium-High) at 1-minute intervals, or until warm, rotating plate and touching bottom center of plate after each minute to determine if food is warm. Microwave your favorite sauces to accompany deep-fried foods.

◄ Coney Dogs

1 lb. ground beef
1 medium onion, chopped
1 can (8 oz.) tomato sauce
¼ cup catsup
1½ teaspoons chili powder
½ teaspoon cayenne
½ teaspoon salt
¼ teaspoon pepper

To serve:
Vegetable oil
8 or 10 hot dogs
8 or 10 hot dog buns

Makes 2 batches
4 or 5 servings each

Crumble ground beef into 2-qt. casserole; add onion. Microwave at High 4 to 6 minutes, or until beef is no longer pink, stirring after half the time to break apart. Drain. Mix in tomato sauce, catsup, chili powder, cayenne, salt and pepper; cover. Microwave at High 13 to 15 minutes, or until spices are blended, stirring every 5 minutes. Divide in half. Freeze half of hamburger mixture (about 1 cup) for later use.

Meanwhile, heat 2 inches of oil to 375°F. in deep-fat fryer or in 3-qt. saucepan on range top. Fry four hot dogs about 1½ minutes, or until deep golden brown. Repeat with remaining four hot dogs. Place in buns; spoon 1 to 2 tablespoons of hamburger mixture over each hot dog.

To defrost reserved hamburger mixture, place in 15-oz. casserole; cover. Microwave at High 3½ to 5½ minutes, or until heated, breaking apart and stirring after half the time. Deep-fry and serve hot dogs as directed, above.

Deep-Fried Cheesy Vegetables

2 cups broccoli flowerets
    or cauliflowerets
2 tablespoons water
¼ cup all-purpose flour
¼ teaspoon salt
⅛ teaspoon pepper
½ lb. pasteurized process
    American cheese loaf,
    cut into 1-in. pieces
½ cup plus 3 tablespoons milk,
    divided
½ cup buttermilk baking mix
¼ teaspoon sugar
    Vegetable oil

Makes 18 pieces

How to Prepare Deep-Fried Cheesy Vegetables

Place broccoli flowerets and water in 2-qt. casserole; cover. Microwave at High 2½ to 3½ minutes, or until tender-crisp, stirring once. (Microwave cauliflowerets 3½ to 4½ minutes.)

Drain vegetables. Set aside. Combine flour, salt and pepper in plastic bag. Add vegetables; shake to coat. Set aside.

Combine cheese and 3 tablespoons milk in 1-qt. casserole. Reduce power to 50% (Medium). Microwave 1 to 2½ minutes, or until smooth, stirring every 30 seconds.

Dip floured vegetables in cheese. Place on wax paper-lined tray. If needed, resoften cheese in bowl by microwaving at 50% (Medium) for 15 seconds. Refrigerate flowerets 30 minutes, or until cheese is firm.

Combine baking mix and sugar in small bowl. Mix in remaining ½ cup milk with fork until smooth. Refrigerate 30 minutes. Heat 2 to 3 inches of oil to 375°F. in deep-fat fryer or in 3-qt. saucepan on range top.

Form cheese around vegetables. Shake in seasoned flour. Dip in batter. Fry, three pieces at a time, 30 to 45 seconds, or until light golden brown, turning over several times during cooking.

Microwave & Food Processor

The microwave oven and the food processor are timesaving appliances that you can use together to make food preparation and cooking even faster. Because small pieces of food microwave faster and more evenly, use the processor to slice vegetables thinly or chop coarsely for microwaved casseroles, soups, sauces or stir-fries. Microwave liver or chicken to process for pâtés and spreads. Microwave vegetables or fruits, then process for purées and cream soups.

Microwave & Food Processor Teamwork

- Shred cheese with the processor to help it melt quickly in microwaved casseroles, sauces or vegetable dishes.
- Make bread crumbs in processor, then dry in the microwave, page 145.
- Microwave a simple syrup, then flavor and freeze it. Process for sorbets, page 73.
- Microwave vegetables and fruit, then process for baby food, page 126.

Cream of Cauliflower Soup ▶

½ cup finely chopped celery
⅓ cup finely chopped onion
2 tablespoons butter or
   margarine
4 cups cauliflowerets
1 can (10¾ oz.) condensed
   chicken broth
1 cup half and half
1 pkg. (4 oz.) shredded
   Cheddar cheese
⅛ teaspoon white pepper

Serves 4

Follow photo directions, below.

Cream of Asparagus Soup

½ cup finely chopped celery
⅓ cup finely chopped onion
2 tablespoons butter or
   margarine
1 lb. fresh asparagus, trimmed
   and chopped
1 can (10¾ oz.) condensed
   chicken broth
1 cup half and half
½ teaspoon curry powder,
   optional

Serves 4

Follow photo directions, below.

How to Prepare Cream Soups

Combine celery, onion and butter in 2-qt. casserole; cover. Microwave at High 5 to 7 minutes, or until tender, stirring once. Add vegetable; cover.

Microwave at High 4 to 7 minutes, or until tender, stirring after half the time. Process in food processor 5 or 6 on/off turns, or until puréed.

Return to casserole. Blend in remaining ingredients. Reduce power to 50% (Medium). Microwave, uncovered, 7 to 11 minutes, or until heated, stirring every 3 minutes.

Softening & Melting

Butter or Margarine

Butter and margarine have a high fat content which attracts microwave energy, so they melt and soften quickly. The secret to getting the desired results is to use the correct power level.

Softening makes butter easy to cream or spread. To soften but not melt, microwave at 30% (Medium-Low). Mix softened butter with flour for thickening sauces; cream it with sweet or savory flavorings to use as a spread. Experiment with your own additions, such as cinnamon and sugar for toast. Or add minced herbs, onions or anchovies to butter; serve with meats, fish or vegetables.

Melting liquifies butter, and is done quickly at High. Melted butter is used in many recipes. Add lemon juice, wine, or minced fresh herbs to melted butter to create sauces for seafood or vegetables.

Butter or Margarine Chart

Amount	Microwave Time
To melt:	**High:**
1 tablespoon	30 - 45 sec.
¼ cup	45 - 60 sec.
½ cup	¾ - 1½ min.
¾ cup	1 - 1½ min.
1 cup	1¼ - 2 min.
To soften:	**30% (Med.-Low):**
½ cup	10 - 50 sec.

Browned Butter. Place ½ cup butter or margarine in microwave-safe plastic dish. (Dish must be oven-safe up to 400°F.) Microwave at High 5 to 6 minutes, or until deep golden brown, stirring every 3 minutes. Skim foam. If desired, stir in 1 teaspoon snipped fresh herbs (parsley, tarragon or basil) and 1 teaspoon lemon juice or white wine vinegar. Serve with eggs, fish, poultry or vegetables.

Clarified Butter. Melt ½ or 1 cup salted or unsalted butter in 12- to 14-oz. shallow casserole as directed in chart, left. Immediately skim foam from surface; reserve. Let butter stand 1 to 2 minutes to allow any remaining solids to settle. Spoon off clear liquid to serve with fish and seafood. White solids can be reserved to toss with vegetables. Refrigerate no longer than 1 week.

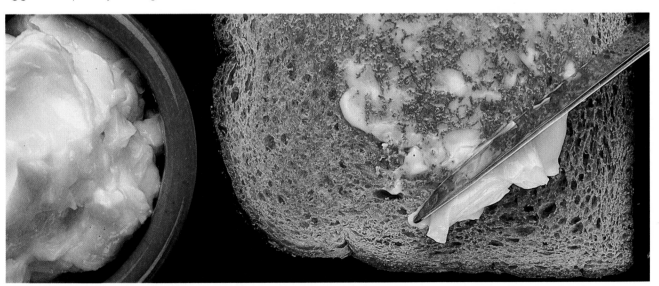

Softened Butter or Margarine. Place ½ cup butter or margarine on serving plate or in bowl.

Microwave at 30% (Medium-Low) 10 to 50 seconds, or until softened, rotating plate every 15

seconds. If butter begins to melt, remove from oven and let stand until softened.

Instant White Sauce

½ cup Softened Butter or
   Margarine, page 39
½ cup all-purpose flour
1 teaspoon salt

¼ teaspoon white pepper
To serve:
  1 cup milk

Makes 4 sauces

Soften butter as directed. In small bowl blend butter, flour, salt and white pepper. Form into four balls, each about 3 tablespoons. Place on wax paper-lined plate or tray. Freeze until firm. Package in plastic bag; seal. Label and freeze no longer than 1 month.

To prepare sauce, place 1 cup milk in 2-cup measure. Unwrap one frozen flour-butter ball and add to milk. Microwave at High 2½ to 4 minutes, or until thickened and bubbly, stirring with fork or wire whip every 30 seconds.

Honey Butter

½ cup Softened Butter or
   Margarine, page 39
⅓ cup honey

Makes ¾ cup

Soften butter as directed. Add honey. Beat with electric mixer until combined. Spread on toast, pancakes, waffles or quick breads. Refrigerate any remaining butter no longer than 2 weeks.

Garlic Butter

¼ cup water
 2 cloves garlic, peeled
½ cup Softened Butter or
   Margarine, page 39

2 tablespoons vegetable oil
1 teaspoon grated Parmesan
   cheese
⅛ teaspoon dry mustard

Makes about ½ cup

Place water and garlic in 1-cup measure. Microwave at High 1 minute, or until boiling. Set aside. Soften butter as directed. Place butter in small bowl. Remove garlic from water; mash with fork. Add to butter. Blend in remaining ingredients with fork, beating until light and fluffy. Serve with meats, hot cooked vegetables or breads. Refrigerate any remaining butter no longer than 2 weeks.

Raspberry Butter

½ cup Softened Butter or
   Margarine, page 39
¾ cup powdered sugar
1 tablespoon raspberry jam

Makes ¾ cup

Soften butter as directed. Mix butter and sugar until smooth and creamy. Blend in raspberry jam. Spread on toast, pancakes, waffles or quick breads. Refrigerate any remaining butter no longer than 2 weeks.

Cheese

Cheese melts rapidly in the microwave oven, but all cheese does not soften and melt at the same rate. You get the best results if you know the difference between the various types of cheese. In general, a very soft and moist cheese melts easily. The longer a cheese is aged, the firmer and drier it becomes, making it more difficult to melt.

The main types of cheese are natural cheese, which may be unripened or aged; process cheese, cheese foods and cheese spreads. Natural cheese provides richer cheese flavor, while process cheese has a milder flavor and melts more easily. Cheese should be shredded or cut into small cubes before adding to sauces or casseroles. Because of its high protein content, cheese toughens and becomes stringy if overheated. Microwave cheese at 50% (Medium); stir frequently.

Semi-Soft Aged Cheese. Brick, Bel Paese and Muenster melt easily when microwaved. Warm cheese, page 44, to serve with crackers or with fruit.

Unripened Natural Cheese. These include soft cheese, cottage, cream and ricotta, which are served cold. Cottage and ricotta cheese are often used in casseroles. Soften cream cheese in the microwave oven for spreading or blending with other ingredients. Mozzarella, a firm unripened cheese, is firm enough to slice or shred and melts easily.

Firm Aged Cheese. These soften and lose their shape when microwaved, but do not melt unless they are mixed with liquids. Some types, such as Colby, Monterey Jack, mild Cheddar or Swiss melt well in casseroles or fondue. Sharp Cheddar is the most difficult to melt and may have a curdled appearance in sauces.

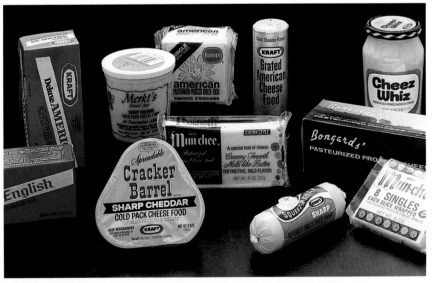

Soft Aged Cheese. Brie, Camembert and Limburger are high in moisture content and melt well. Serve them slightly warmed or melted, page 44, to add an elegant touch as an appetizer or dessert.

Process Cheese/Process Cheese Food & Spread. Process cheese melts easily and blends smoothly into microwaved soups, sauces or casseroles. It is blended from a combination of unripened and aged natural cheese, and then pasteurized to prevent further aging. Popular flavors are American, Swiss and Brick. Process cheese food and spread melt faster than process cheese. They contain more moisture but less cheese and milk fat. They are packaged in slices, loaves, jars and rolls.

Soften Cream Cheese. Use your microwave to soften cream cheese to ease blending for use in your favorite appetizer, main dish or dessert recipe. Also, soften for easier spreading. Cream cheese can be softened directly on microwave-safe serving dish. Do not microwave cream cheese in the foil wrapper. Soften as directed in chart, below.

Warm Soft Aged Cheese.
Warm cheeses such as Brie or Camembert to serving temperature by microwaving as directed in chart, below. Cheese can be microwaved directly on wooden serving tray.

Cheese Chart

Item	Microwave Time at 30% (Med.-Low)	Procedure
To warm: Firm Aged Cheese ½ lb.	30 - 45 sec.	Place on serving dish. Microwave until slightly warm to touch. Rotate after half the time. Let stand 5 minutes.
Soft and Semi-Soft Aged Cheese ½ lb.	15 - 45 sec.	Place on serving dish. Microwave until slightly warm to touch. Rotate after half the time. Let stand 5 minutes.
To soften: Cream Cheese 3 oz. 8 oz.	**50% (Med.)** 30 - 60 sec. 1 - 1½ min.	Remove from foil, place in shallow dish. Microwave until cheese is softened.

Warm Firm Aged Cheese.
Enhance the flavor of cheeses such as Cheddar, Colby or Monterey Jack by microwaving as directed in chart, left. Cheese can be microwaved directly on wooden serving tray.

Layered Cheese Loaf ►

½ pkg. (8 oz.) cream cheese
2 tablespoons butter or
    margarine
½ teaspoon dried basil leaves
    or dry mustard
3 slices Colby cheese,
    3½ × 3½-in.
3 slices brick cheese,
    3½ × 3½-in.
1 slice (¾ oz.) salami
2 tablespoons snipped fresh
    parsley

Makes one ¾-lb. loaf

Place cream cheese and butter in small bowl. Microwave at 30% (Medium-Low) 15 to 60 seconds, or until softened, rotating every 15 seconds. Blend in basil. On serving plate layer cheese slices and salami, spreading about 2 teaspoons of cream cheese mixture between each layer. Use remaining cream cheese mixture to spread on top and sides. Sprinkle with parsley, pressing gently to coat loaf. Refrigerate at least 3 hours before serving. Serve with crackers, if desired.

Cheese Sauce   Pictured on page 42

2 tablespoons butter or
    margarine
⅛ teaspoon salt
2 tablespoons all-purpose flour
1 cup milk
1 cup shredded cheese
    (Jalapeño, caraway, onion,
    garlic or dill)

Makes 1½ cups

Place butter and salt in 4-cup measure. Microwave at High 30 to 45 seconds, or until butter melts. Blend in flour; stir in milk. Microwave at High 3 to 4 minutes, or until thickened, stirring with fork or wire whip after each minute. Add cheese, stirring until melted. Serve hot over cooked vegetables, or cover and chill to serve as a dip for raw vegetables.

Crock Cheese

1 lb. Cheddar, Colby or
  Monterey Jack cheese
½ cup butter or margarine
1 pkg. (3 oz.) cream cheese

2 tablespoons finely chopped
  onion
1 to 2 tablespoons butter or
  margarine, melted, page 38

Makes 1½ pounds

Flavor Variations:

Port Wine Cheese: Add ¼ cup port or sherry wine, 2 tablespoons snipped fresh parsley, ¼ teaspoon fresh ground pepper and ⅛ teaspoon garlic powder to the softened cheese and butter mixture. Continue as directed.

Pepper Cheese: Add 1 tablespoon finely chopped fresh or canned jalapeño pepper and ½ teaspoon dried crushed red pepper flakes to the softened cheese and butter mixture. Continue as directed.

Pepperoni Cheese: Add ⅓ cup finely chopped pepperoni to the softened cheese and butter mixture. Continue as directed.

NOTE: Crock Cheese mixture can be divided in half and given two flavors by following two of the flavor variations, using half the amounts indicated.

How to Microwave Crock Cheese

Cut cheese, butter and cream cheese into 1-in. pieces. Place in medium bowl. Microwave at 30% (Medium-Low) 1 to 3½ minutes, or until slightly softened, stirring and rotating bowl every 30 seconds. Watch carefully to avoid melting.

Mash the cheese and the butter pieces with a fork or pastry blender until smooth.

Stir in onion. Add any flavor variation ingredients, as desired.

Pack mixture into cheese crock, serving dish, cellophane-lined clay pot, mug or pitcher.

Pour melted butter over cheese to seal crock (⅛-in. layer). Refrigerate cheese no longer than 2 weeks.

Cheese Ball or Log

Crock Cheese, opposite

Coatings:

1 cup finely chopped walnuts plus ¼ cup snipped fresh parsley

1 cup finely crushed corn chips

¼ cup Toasted Sesame Seed, page 91

Makes 2 cheese balls or 2 cheese logs

Prepare Crock Cheese as directed, but do not pack in crock. Divide cheese mixture in half. Shape into two 3½-in. diameter balls or two 6-in. logs. Roll in one of the coatings. Refrigerate at least 3 hours, or until firm. Store in refrigerator no longer than 1 week.

Cheese Soup

3 tablespoons butter or margarine

⅓ cup chopped onion

¼ cup grated carrot

2 tablespoons sliced almonds, chopped

¼ cup all-purpose flour

¼ teaspoon white pepper

⅛ teaspoon salt

1½ cups milk

1 can (10¾ oz.) condensed chicken broth

2 cups shredded pasteurized process cheese spread loaf with bacon

Serves 4

In 2-qt. casserole combine butter, onion, carrot and almonds. Microwave at High 3 to 4 minutes, or until butter melts and almonds are light brown, stirring after each minute. Stir in flour, pepper and salt. Slowly stir in milk and chicken broth. Microwave at High 7 to 8 minutes, or until slightly thickened, stirring every 2 minutes. Add cheese, stirring to melt. Garnish with pretzels, if desired.

Chocolate

The microwave oven melts chocolate like magic; you'll never want to do it by any other method. There's little danger of scorching, and no need for a double boiler. If the chocolate becomes too cool for working, you can easily rewarm it.

Chocolate is delicate; never overheat it. Microwave at 50% (Medium) and stir often.

Chocolate is available in many types, which differ in percent of chocolate, cocoa butter, and the other ingredients added. Make sure you have the right type for your purpose.

Melt Chocolate

Fully melted chocolate may hold its shape; if you judge by appearance alone, it can become too hot. The last small pieces should be stirred to melt them completely.

Unsweetened or semi-sweet baking chocolate is rich in chocolate and cocoa butter, and it is used in baking.

Candy coatings are used for dipping or to make bark candy; this chocolate is sold in two grades.

Confectioner's candy coating, which is sold in supermarkets, is lower in cost, but needs the addition of shortening to smooth it to dipping consistency.

Chocolate-flavored candy coating, sometimes referred to as "summer coating," is sold in specialty shops and contains cocoa butter. It has a rich flavor and excellent consistency for dipping, but is more expensive.

Sweet baking chocolate contains less chocolate than unsweetened or semi-sweet baking chocolate, and is also used in baking, or for making decorative garnishes.

Milk chocolate is similar to sweet baking chocolate, but contains additional milk fat and solids. Melted milk chocolate makes a quick dessert topping.

Chocolate chips are either semi-sweet or milk chocolate. Chocolate-flavored chips contain less chocolate and cocoa butter. Chocolate chips are used in baking.

Melt Baking Chocolate. Place desired amount of unsweetened, semi-sweet, or sweet baking chocolate in small bowl. Microwave at 50% (Medium) as directed in chart, below, or until chocolate is glossy and can be stirred smooth, stirring every 2 minutes, then after each minute. Chocolate may hold its shape until stirred. If small amount remains unmelted, continue to stir until melted.

Melt Chocolate Candy Bar. Break one (1.45 oz.) bar into pieces. Place in 1-cup measure or small bowl. Microwave at 50% (Medium) 1½ to 2 minutes, or until chocolate is glossy and can be stirred smooth.

Melt Candy Coating. Break 1 lb. candy coating into pieces. Place in single layer in 2-qt. casserole. Microwave at 50% (Medium) 3 to 5 minutes, or until pieces are glossy and can be stirred smooth. Stir after half the time.

Chocolate Melting Chart

Item	Microwave Time at 50% (Medium)
Chocolate Chips 1 cup	2½ - 3½ min.
Baking Chocolate	
4 squares	2½ - 4 min.
2 squares	2½ - 3½ min.
1 square (1 oz.)	2½ - 4½ min.
½ square	2 - 2½ min.
Milk Chocolate Candy Bar 1.45 oz.	1½ - 2 min.
Sweet Chocolate 4 oz. block	2½ - 4 min.
Candy Coating 1 lb.	3 - 5 min.

Melt Chocolate Chips. Place 1 cup milk chocolate, semi-sweet or chocolate-flavored chips in 1-cup measure. Microwave at 50% (Medium) 2½ to 3½ minutes, stirring as soon as chips begin to melt, then after each minute, or until chocolate is glossy and can be stirred smooth.

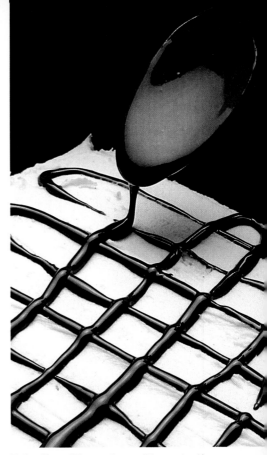

Mint Pattie Icing. Top each of six unfrosted cupcakes or sugar cookies with one chocolate, cream-filled mint pattie. Place in circle on plate. Microwave at 50% (Medium) 1½ to 2 minutes, or until chocolate mint patties are glossy, rotating plate every 30 seconds. Mint patties will continue to hold their shape. With metal spatula, spread softened pattie. Let cool to set.

Chocolate Curls. Place half of 4-oz. block sweet baking chocolate on plate. Microwave at 30% (Medium-Low) 30 to 60 seconds, or until just barely warm to the touch, rotating and turning piece over once. To form curls, hold chocolate upright on its edge. With vegetable peeler, pull toward you across edge of chocolate, in continuous, even motion.

Drizzling Chocolate. Place half of 1-oz. square semi-sweet baking chocolate in custard cup. Add ½ teaspoon shortening. Microwave at 50% (Medium) 2 to 3 minutes, or until chocolate is glossy and can be stirred smooth. Chocolate may hold its shape until stirred. Drizzle from spoon over cakes, candies or pastries.

Bark Candy. Break 1 lb. confectioners' coating or candy coating into pieces. Place in single layer in 2-qt. casserole. Microwave at 50% (Medium) 3 to 5 minutes, or until pieces are glossy and can be stirred smooth, stirring after 3 minutes. If desired, mix in almonds, crushed peppermint candies, raisins or crisp rice cereal. Spread to ¼-in. thickness on foil-lined baking sheet. Cool until firm. Break into pieces. Store in airtight wax paper-lined container.

Chocolate Fantasies

Use the following recipes to decorate glamorous cakes. Top the easiest frosting you ever made with a cluster of glossy chocolate leaves.

Sour Cream Chocolate Frosting ▶

½ cup semi-sweet chocolate
    chips
½ cup dairy sour cream

> Frosts 8 × 8-in. square
> or 9-in. round cake

Place chocolate chips in 1-cup measure or small bowl. Microwave at 50% (Medium) 3 to 3½ minutes, stirring after each minute, or until chips are glossy and can be stirred smooth. Blend in the sour cream, one-third at a time. Refrigerate cake after frosting.

Chocolate Leaves ▶

¼ cup semi-sweet chocolate
    chips
2 teaspoons shortening
8 medium or 12 small fresh
    lemon or rose leaves,
    well-washed

> Makes 1 dozen leaves

How to Microwave Chocolate Leaves

Place chocolate chips and shortening in 1-cup measure. Microwave at 50% (Medium) 2½ to 3 minutes, stirring after 1 minute and then every 30 seconds, or until chips are glossy and can be stirred smooth.

Brush thin layer of chocolate on top side of leaves with a small paintbrush.

Place coated leaves on flat plate. Freeze about 30 minutes, or until chocolate is firm.

Peel the leaf from the chocolate carefully. Return chocolate leaves to freezer or refrigerator until ready to use. Use as garnish on desserts, cakes or pies.

Chocolate Dessert & Liqueur Cups

Dessert Cups:
12 paper cupcake liners
4 squares (1 oz. each) semi-
 sweet baking chocolate
2 teaspoons shortening

Makes 6 dessert cups

Liqueur Cups:
20 paper candy cups
2 squares (1 oz. each) semi-
 sweet baking chocolate
1 teaspoon shortening

Makes 10 liqueur cups

How to Microwave Chocolate Dessert & Liqueur Cups

Double paper liners to yield six dessert cup forms or ten liqueur cup forms. Arrange on flat plate. Set aside. Place desired amount of chocolate and short-ening in 2-cup measure.

Microwave at 50% (Medium) 3½ to 4 minutes (dessert cups) or 2½ to 3½ minutes (liqueur cups), or until mixture is glossy and can be stirred smooth, stirring after each minute.

Spoon 1 tablespoon melted chocolate into each double thickness dessert cup liner or 1 teaspoon melted chocolate into each liqueur cup form. Tilt cups to coat sides to within ⅛ inch of top. Continue to tilt to form thick chocolate shell.

Return coated liners to flat plate. Refrigerate dessert cups 1 hour before removing paper, and liqueur cups 30 minutes. Return to refrigerator until serving time. Fill dessert cups with sherbet or ice cream; fill liqueur cups with liqueurs.

Melting Chocolate

Use your microwave whenever a recipe calls for melted chocolate. No double boiler is needed because microwave energy penetrates from all sides rather than just the base as in range-top cooking. Microwaving also eliminates the need for constant stirring and reduces the possibility of scorching.

Chocolate Dipped Snacks & Fruit

Coating:
½ lb. chocolate-flavored candy coating or white candy coating

Or:
½ lb. confectioners' candy coating plus 1 tablespoon shortening

Dippers:
Potato chips, broken into 1- to 1½-in. pieces
Pretzels
Candied Peel, page 89
Candied Pineapple, page 88
Fresh strawberries

Makes about 6 dozen pieces

Place candy coating in 2-cup measure or small deep bowl. Microwave at 50% (Medium) 3 to 4½ minutes, or until coating is glossy and can be stirred smooth, rotating after each minute. Stir to melt any small pieces. If coating begins to set, resoften at 50% (Medium) at 1-minute intervals, or until of proper dipping consistency.

Use two forks to dip pieces into coating. Let excess coating fall back into bowl. Cool on wire rack until set. Store pretzels or potato chips in wax paper-lined container in cool, dry place. Refrigerate chocolate-coated fruit until serving time.

Miscellaneous

The microwave oven's ability to soften and melt can simplify and enhance food preparation in many ways. Turn jelly or jam into a quick and colorful meat glaze or dessert topping. Restore hardened brown sugar, crystallized honey, even over-set gelatin.

Soften ice cream and blend with your favorite liqueur to create your own liqueur-flavored specialties or mold a dramatic ice cream dessert.

Miscellaneous Softening Chart (see photo directions)

Item	Microwave Time at High
Tostada & Taco Shells	
2 shells	15 - 20 sec.
4 shells	25 - 30 sec.
6 shells	30 - 45 sec.
8 shells	45 - 60 sec.
Tortillas, 4 to 6	20 - 40 sec.
Jelly & Jam	
¼ cup	30 - 45 sec.
½ cup	1 - 1¼ min.
1 cup	1½ - 2 min.
Ice Cream Topping	
¼ cup	25 - 35 sec.
½ cup	40 - 60 sec.
1 cup	1 - 1¼ min.
Peanut Butter	
¼ or ½ cup	30 - 60 sec.
Ice Cream	**50% (Med.):**
1 quart	30 - 60 sec.
½ gallon	1 min.
Overset Gelatin	**50% (Med.):**
3-oz. pkg.	1 - 1½ min.
6-oz. pkg.	1 - 2 min.

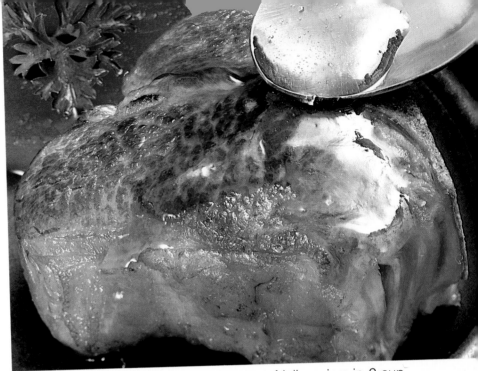

Warm Tostada & Taco Shells. Place stack of shells on roasting rack. Microwave at High as directed in chart, left, until hot and slightly softened.

Melt Jelly & Jam. Place desired amount of jelly or jam in 2-cup measure or medium bowl. Microwave at High as directed in chart, left, or until melted, stirring every 30 seconds. Serve as dessert topping, as a glaze for meats, or use for sauces.

Soften Hard Brown Sugar. Sprinkle brown sugar lightly with water or add one apple slice to bag. Close bag loosely with string. Microwave at High 30 to 60 seconds, checking after half the time. Let stand 5 minutes to complete softening. If brown sugar begins to melt, remove from oven and let stand to complete softening. For amounts less than ½ lb., microwave at High until softened, checking every 15 seconds.

Soften & Warm Tortillas. Place four to six flour or corn tortillas between damp paper towels. Microwave at High 20 to 40 seconds, or until tortillas are warm to the touch.

Soften Ice Cream. To soften ice cream for scooping individual servings, or for layering in desserts, microwave in cardboard container at 50% (Medium) about 30 seconds. Scoop out desired amount; re-freeze remaining ice cream in container.

Soften ice cream for filling pies or cakes, or for creating liqueur-flavored ice creams. Remove 1 quart ice cream from container. Place in medium bowl. Cut into quarters. Microwave at 50% (Medium) 30 to 60 seconds, or until softened.

Liqueur-Flavored Ice Cream. Stir ¼ cup liqueur into 1 quart softened ice cream, above. Place in freezer for 1 hour. Stir again, cover with foil, and store in freezer until serving time.

Flavor Combinations:
- Coffee Liqueur, page 103, with chocolate, vanilla or coffee ice cream
- Crème de Menthe, page 102, with chocolate ice cream
- Orange Liqueur, page 102, with chocolate or coffee ice cream
- Raspberry Liqueur, page 103, with peach or chocolate ice cream

Praline Ice Cream. Stir 1 cup crushed Orange-Spiced Pecan Brittle, page 93, into 1 quart softened ice cream and freeze as directed for Liqueur-Flavored Ice Cream, above.

Warm Ice Cream Topping.
Spoon desired amount of ice cream topping (butterscotch, fudge, chocolate, pineapple, caramel or strawberry) into 2-cup measure or small bowl. Microwave at High as directed in the chart, page 56, until heated. Stir. Serve over ice cream or cake.

Prepare Gelatin. Measure water as directed on package. Microwave 1 cup at High 2 to 3 minutes, or 2 cups 3 to 5 minutes, or until boiling. Stir in gelatin until dissolved. Add cold water.

Soften Overset Gelatin. If gelatin sets before you have added fruit, vegetables or nuts, resoften it. Microwave at 50% (Medium) 1 to 1½ minutes for 3-oz. package or 1 to 2 minutes for 6-oz. package, or until soft-set. Stir. Add desired ingredients. Refrigerate until firm.

Soften Crystallized Honey.
Remove lid from glass honey bottle, or transfer from plastic container to measuring cup. Microwave at High 2 to 2½ minutes, or until clear, stirring every 30 seconds. Let cool.

Soften Peanut Butter. To ease spreading, microwave ¼ or ½ cup peanut butter at High 30 seconds, or until easy to stir. For a dessert sauce, continue to microwave additional 30 seconds, or until of a thin consistency. Serve over chocolate ice cream.

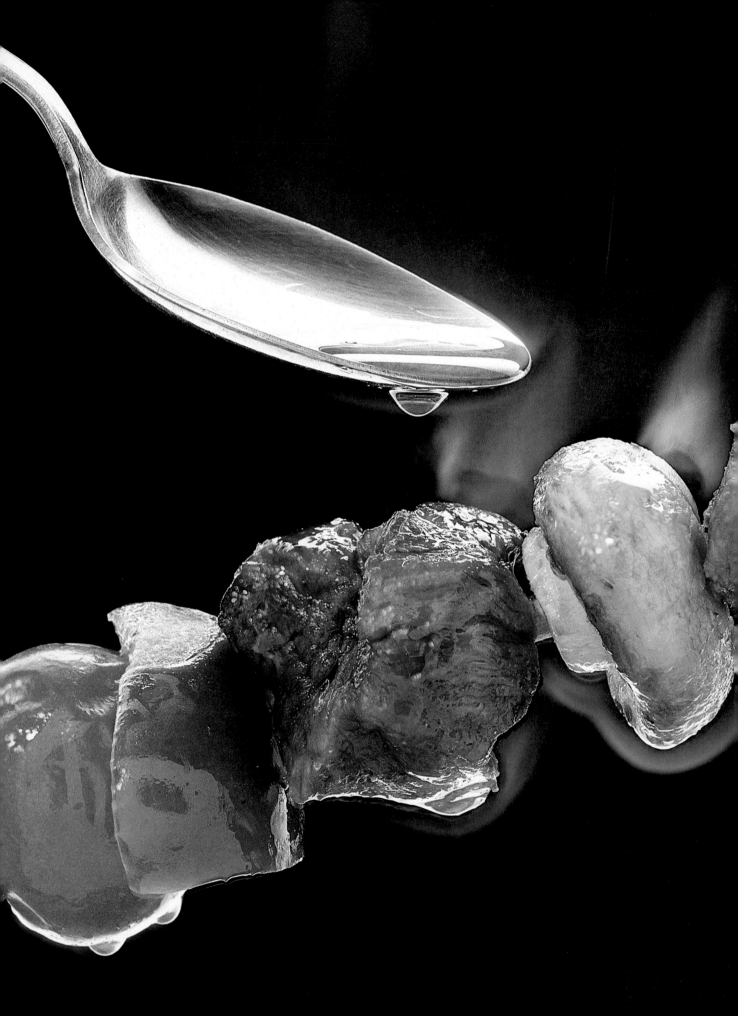

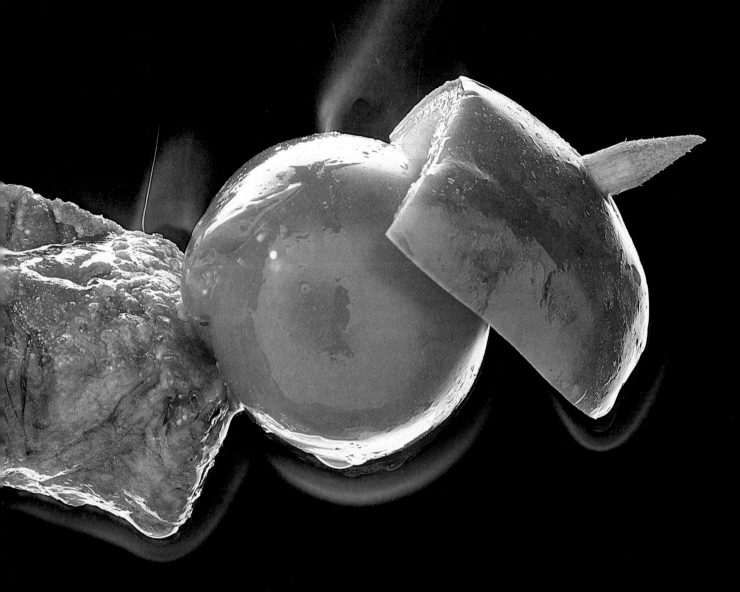

Easy & Elegant

Elegant cooking is not only for people with plenty of time and special skills. Learn how to create special effects quickly and easily with your microwave oven. Because of the difference in cooking methods, conventional dishes which are time-consuming and fussy can be fast and easy with microwaving.

Beautiful vegetable presentations, like the classic Bouquetière, are good examples. Conventionally, each vegetable in the bouquet must be cooked separately and arranged in artistic clusters at the last moment. The microwave technique is to assemble an eye-pleasing still life of assorted vegetables *before* cooking. You can even do it early in the day. The vegetables are arranged to look dramatic and to microwave in the same amount of time.

Try these microwave versions of the classic sauces, refreshing sorbets to serve between courses, as well as hors d'oeuvres, entrées, vegetable garnishes and desserts to give gourmet flair to any occasion.

Seafood Au Gratin

2 tablespoons butter or
   margarine
2 tablespoons chopped green
   onion
2 tablespoons all-purpose flour
¼ teaspoon salt
⅛ teaspoon white pepper
   Dash cayenne
1 cup whipping cream

1 tablespoon white wine
¼ cup chopped fresh
   mushrooms
1 pkg. (6 oz.) frozen crab meat,
   defrosted and drained
2 tablespoons grated
   Parmesan cheese
½ cup shredded Cheddar
   cheese

Serves 4

In 4-cup measure combine butter and green onion. Microwave at High 45 to 60 seconds, or until butter is melted. Add flour, salt, white pepper and cayenne. Stir in cream, wine and mushrooms. Reduce power to 50% (Medium). Microwave 4 to 6 minutes, or until thickened, stirring after 2 minutes and then after each minute. Mix in crab meat and Parmesan cheese.

Divide between four baking shells or ramekins. Sprinkle with Cheddar cheese. Microwave at 50% (Medium) 3 to 5 minutes, or until cheese melts, rearranging after half the time. Garnish with parsley sprigs and lemon twists, if desired.

Frosted Pâté ►

1 lb. chicken livers
½ cup shredded carrot
¼ cup chopped onion
¼ cup butter or margarine
2 tablespoons sweet white
    wine
½ teaspoon salt
¼ teaspoon pepper
¼ teaspoon dry mustard
2 pkgs. (3 oz. each) cream
    cheese
2 tablespoons snipped fresh
    parsley

Makes 2 cups

Cut piece of wax paper to fit bottom of 2-cup mold. Butter sides of mold. Rinse chicken livers and drain well. Place in 1½-qt. casserole. Add carrot, onion, butter, wine, salt, pepper and mustard; cover. Microwave at High 5 minutes, stirring after half the time. Reduce power to 50% (Medium). Microwave 3 to 7 minutes, or until chicken livers are no longer pink, stirring after half the time. Place in food processor and blend until smooth. Spoon into prepared 2-cup mold. Refrigerate at least 4 hours. Unmold onto serving plate.

Place cream cheese in small bowl. Microwave at 50% (Medium) 45 seconds to 1¼ minutes, or until softened. Stir in parsley. Frost unmolded pâté. Refrigerate 30 minutes before serving. Serve with crackers, bread sticks or French bread.

Kabob Shielding

Arrange green pepper pieces to curve around cherry tomatoes on kabobs. Peppers will shield the tomatoes and prevent them from splitting.

Shish Kabob Pictured on page 60

Marinade:
⅔ cup white wine
⅓ cup vegetable oil
1 small onion, sliced
1 clove garlic, peeled and cut
    in half
¼ teaspoon dried bouquet
    garni seasoning
¼ teaspoon salt
⅛ teaspoon freshly cracked
    black pepper
2 teaspoons Worcestershire
    sauce

Kabobs:
1½ lbs. beef boneless sirloin,
    cut into 16 chunks
1 large green pepper, cut into
    16 pieces
4 wooden skewers, 12-in.
    long
8 cherry tomatoes
4 large mushroom caps

¼ cup brandy

Serves 4

In medium bowl or 2-qt. casserole combine marinade ingredients. Add meat. Toss to coat with marinade. Cover. Refrigerate at least 4 hours, turning meat over after half the time.

Place green pepper in 1-qt. casserole or small bowl. Cover. Microwave at High 1 to 2 minutes, or until tender-crisp, stirring after half the time. Set aside.

Assemble kabobs on skewers, alternating meat with vegetables. Place kabobs on microwave roasting rack or baking sheet. Cover with wax paper. Reduce power to 50% (Medium). Microwave 9 to 12 minutes, or until desired doneness, rotating roasting rack every 3 minutes, and rearranging kabobs after half the time. Set aside.

To serve, place brandy in small bowl or custard cup. Microwave at High 30 seconds, or until bowl is warm to touch. Ignite brandy and spoon over kabobs. Serve kabobs on bed of rice, if desired.

◄ Lemon Studded Artichokes

4 whole fresh artichokes
8 thin lemon slices
  Melted butter, page 38,
  optional

Serves 4

Trim each artichoke 2 inches from top and close to base so they will stand upright. Snap off small lower leaves. Snip tips of outer leaves. Rinse; shake off excess water. Cut two lemon slices into eight wedges and tuck into outer leaves of one artichoke with lemon peel showing. Repeat with remaining lemon slices and artichokes.

Wrap each artichoke in plastic wrap. Microwave at High 9½ to 14½ minutes, or until lower leaves can be easily pulled off and base is fork tender, rotating and rearranging after half the time. Serve with melted butter.

NOTE: For two servings, use two artichokes and four thin lemon slices. Prepare as directed, above. Microwave at High 5½ to 8½ minutes.

Butter-Braised Vegetables ▲

2 medium baking potatoes,
  peeled and quartered
3 medium carrots, cut into
  2½- to 3-in. lengths
2 stalks celery, cut into
  2½- to 3-in. lengths
¼ cup water
  Browned Butter, page 39

Serves 4

Combine potatoes, carrots and celery in 2-qt. casserole. Add water; cover. Microwave at High 8 to 11 minutes, or until fork tender, stirring after half the time. Let stand 5 minutes.

Prepare Browned Butter as directed. Drain vegetables; toss with Browned Butter.

Glamour Garnish

Use any of these recipes to garnish a meat platter. Place carved meat in center of microwave-safe platter. Garnish with desired vegetables. Microwave at 70% (Medium-High), checking after each minute, until meat and vegetables are reheated.

Stuffed Mushrooms ▲

8 whole fresh mushrooms, 2½-
  to 3-in. diameter
2 tablespoons butter or
  margarine or Garlic Butter,
  page 41
1 tablespoon sherry
½ teaspoon salt
⅛ teaspoon pepper
4 oz. Camembert or Muenster
  cheese
8 fresh parsley sprigs

Serves 4

Brush mushrooms to clean. Trim
⅛ inch off stem end. Remove
stems and chop fine. Arrange
caps in 12 × 8-in. baking dish,
stem side up. Set aside.

In 1-qt. casserole combine
chopped stems, butter and
sherry. Microwave at High 1½
to 2½ minutes, or until tender.
Stir in salt and pepper. Mound
in mushroom caps. Cut eight
pieces of cheese and place on
top of stuffed mushrooms.

Reduce power to 50%
(Medium). Microwave 5 to 6½
minutes, or until cheese melts,
rotating dish and rearranging
mushrooms after half the time.
Top each with sprig of parsley.
Let stand 5 minutes.

Tomato-Capped Onions ▶

2 medium onions, peeled
2 medium tomatoes, peeled,
  page 86
2 tablespoons water
1 tablespoon butter or
  margarine
1 teaspoon snipped fresh
  parsley
  Dash white pepper
2 teaspoons grated Parmesan
  cheese

Serves 4

Choose onions and tomatoes
similar in size. Cut onions in half
crosswise. Place in 1-qt. casserole. Sprinkle with water. Cover.
Microwave at High 3½ to 5 minutes, or until fork tender, rotating
casserole after half the time.
Place onions on plate. Cut out
stem end of tomatoes and cut
in half lengthwise; place on
onion halves.

Melt butter in 1-cup measure at
High 30 to 45 seconds. Stir in
parsley and pepper. Spoon
over the tomato-topped onions.
Microwave at High 3 to 5 minutes, or until tomatoes are fork
tender, rotating plate once.
Sprinkle ½ teaspoon cheese on
top of each tomato.

Vegetable Arrangement

Arrangement is the secret of microwaving several foods with different cooking times. Place longer-cooking items around the edge of the platter. Make a second ring of vegetables with medium cooking times. Quick-cooking vegetables go in the center, where they receive less energy. The vegetables cook evenly and look beautiful.

◀ Garden Bouquet Vegetable Platter

1 lb. fresh asparagus, trimmed
4 oz. fresh whole mushrooms, 1-in. diameter
½ lb. yellow squash, cut into ½-in. slices
1 medium zucchini, cut into 2½ × ¼-in. strips
1 medium carrot, cut into 2½ × ¼-in. strips
2 tablespoons water
1 whole pimiento
Browned Butter, page 39

Serves 6 to 8

Arrange asparagus spears in center of 12- to 14-in. round microwave-safe platter. Arrange mushrooms, squash, zucchini and carrots around spears, alternating colors and types of vegetables. Sprinkle with water. Cover with plastic wrap.

Microwave at High 8 to 9 minutes, or until tender-crisp, rotating platter 2 times during cooking. Feel through wrap to test doneness; vegetables should feel soft to the touch and pliable. Let stand 5 minutes. Cut pimiento into spiral strip and form a bow. Garnish asparagus spears with pimiento bow. Prepare Browned Butter as directed. Serve with vegetables.

Elegant Vegetable Platter ▲

1 artichoke
½ lb. fresh carrots, cut into 2½ × ¼-in. strips
4 cups fresh cauliflowerets
8 oz. fresh Brussels sprouts, trimmed and cut in half
2 tablespoons water
Cheese Sauce, page 45

Serves 6 to 8

Trim artichoke 2 inches from top and close to base so it will stand upright. Snap off small lower leaves. Snip tips of outer leaves. Rinse; shake off excess water. Wrap in plastic wrap. Microwave at High 3 minutes. Remove plastic and place artichoke at one end of microwave-safe platter.

Place carrots in center of platter. Arrange cauliflowerets and Brussels sprouts around edge, alternating clusters of vegetables for color effect. Sprinkle water over vegetables. Cover platter with plastic wrap. Microwave at High 8 to 11 minutes, or until tender-crisp, rotating platter 2 times. Feel through wrap to test doneness; vegetables should feel soft to the touch and pliable. Let stand 5 minutes. Prepare Cheese Sauce as directed. Serve with vegetable platter.

Whole Cauliflower

Wash a 1-lb. head of cauliflower. Shake off water. Wrap in plastic wrap. Place on serving plate upside down. Microwave at High 3 minutes. Turn over. Microwave at High 2½ to 4½ minutes, or until base is fork tender. Let stand, covered, 3 minutes. Serve with Cheese Sauce, page 45.

Broccoli & Cauliflower Ring ▲

1 small tomato, cut into 6
    wedges and seeded
4 cups fresh broccoli flowerets
4 cups fresh cauliflowerets
¼ cup water
¼ cup butter or margarine
1 tablespoon fresh lemon juice
¼ teaspoon salt
⅛ teaspoon pepper

Serves 6 to 8

Arrange tomato wedges skin side down on bottom of 6-cup glass ring mold. Set aside. Place broccoli flowerets and cauliflowerets in 3-qt. casserole. Sprinkle water over vegetables; cover. Microwave at High 9 to 13 minutes, or until tender-crisp; stirring after half the time. Drain.

Arrange vegetables over tomatoes in mold, pressing to pack firmly. Set aside. Place butter in 1-cup measure. Microwave at High 45 to 60 seconds, or until melted. Blend in lemon juice, salt and pepper. Pour lemon butter over vegetables. Microwave molded vegetables at High 3 minutes. Invert onto serving plate.

Cauliflower With Carrots & New Potatoes

½ cup Browned Butter,
    page 39
2 lb. head fresh cauliflower
¾ lb. new potatoes
12 oz. fresh tiny carrots,
    scrubbed or peeled
1 medium onion, cut into
    8 wedges
2 tablespoons water

Serves 6 to 8

Prepare Browned Butter as directed. Set aside. Trim cauliflower at base. Rinse. Place base-side up at one end of 14-in. oval or 12-in. round microwave-safe platter.

Remove thin strip of peel from around middle of each potato. Toss potatoes, carrots and onions in Browned Butter. Set aside remaining Browned Butter. Arrange potatoes around edge of platter. Arrange carrots to fan around plate. Place onions in center. Sprinkle with water. Cover with plastic wrap.

Microwave at High 12 to 16 minutes, or until vegetables are fork tender, rotating platter 2 times and turning cauliflower right side up after half the time. Let stand 5 minutes. Serve with remaining Browned Butter.

Broccoli & Carrot Platter ▶

2 lbs. fresh broccoli
1 lb. fresh carrots, peeled
2 tablespoons water
    Browned Butter, page 39, or
    Cheese Sauce, page 45

Serves 6 to 8

Separate broccoli flowerets from stalks. Set aside. Trim 1 inch from ends of stalks and discard. Peel stalks. Shred stalk in food processor. Arrange shredded broccoli in center of 12- or 14-in. round microwave-safe platter. Surround with flowerets.

Roll-cut carrots by holding flat on cutting board. Make diagonal cut straight down. Roll carrot ¼ turn and cut again. Pieces should be about 1½ inches long. Arrange near edge of platter around flowerets. Sprinkle water over vegetables. Cover with plastic wrap.

Microwave at High 10 to 14 minutes, or until carrots are fork tender, rotating platter 2 times. Prepare Browned Butter or Cheese Sauce as directed. Serve with vegetables.

Béchamel Sauce

2 tablespoons butter or
   margarine
2 teaspoons minced onion
2 tablespoons all-purpose flour
¼ teaspoon salt
   Dash white pepper
1 cup half and half
1 small bay leaf

Makes about 1 cup

Place butter and onion in 2-cup
measure. Microwave at High 1
to 1½ minutes, or until tender.
Stir in flour, salt and white pepper. Blend in half and half. Add
bay leaf. Reduce power to 50%
(Medium). Microwave 5 to 6½
minutes, or until thickened, stirring after each minute with wire
whip. Discard bay leaf. Serve
with poultry, pasta or vegetables.

Easy Béarnaise Sauce

3 egg yolks
1 teaspoon white vinegar
1 teaspoon white wine
½ teaspoon dried tarragon
   leaves

⅛ teaspoon salt
   Dash white pepper
½ cup butter or margarine
1 tablespoon minced onion

Makes ¾ cup

Combine egg yolks, vinegar, wine, tarragon, salt and white pepper
in blender or food processor. Blend about 5 seconds, or until
smooth. Place butter and onion in 2-cup measure. Microwave at
High 45 seconds to 1¼ minutes, or until butter is melted and
bubbly. Continue to blend egg yolks at low speed, adding hot
butter and onion in slow and steady stream until sauce thickens.
Serve immediately with fish or beef.

Easy Sauce

In the microwave oven, energy penetrates sauces from all
directions, so they cook faster and require little stirring to
achieve a smooth consistency. For easy clean-up, measure, mix
and microwave in a measuring cup.

Hollandaise Sauce

3 egg yolks
1 tablespoon plus 1½ tea-
    spoons fresh lemon juice
⅛ teaspoon salt
    Dash white pepper
½ cup butter or margarine

Makes ⅔ cup

Combine egg yolks, lemon
juice, salt and white pepper in
blender or food processor.
Blend about 5 seconds, or until
smooth. Place butter in 2-cup
measure. Microwave at High 45
seconds to 1¼ minutes, or until
melted and bubbly. Continue to
blend egg yolk mixture at low
speed, adding hot butter in
slow and steady stream until
sauce thickens. Serve immediately with vegetables or eggs.

Mornay Sauce

2 tablespoons butter or
    margarine
2 tablespoons all-purpose flour
1 teaspoon snipped fresh
    parsley
½ teaspoon instant chicken
    bouillon granules
    Dash white pepper
1 cup half and half
¼ cup shredded Swiss cheese
2 tablespoons grated
    Parmesan cheese

Makes 1¼ cups

Place butter in 2-cup measure. Microwave at High 30 to 45
seconds, or until melted. Stir in flour, parsley, bouillon granules and
white pepper. Blend in half and half.

Reduce power to 50% (Medium). Microwave 4 to 6 minutes, or
until thickened, stirring after each minute with fork or wire whip. Stir
in cheeses until melted. Serve immediately with vegetables.

◀ French Strawberry Glacé Pie

One-Crust Pastry Shell,
  page 23
1 pkg. (8 oz.) cream cheese,
  softened, page 44
¼ cup sugar
1 qt. fresh strawberries,
  washed and hulled
1 cup strawberry preserves

Makes 9-in. pie

Prepare pie shell as directed; cool. Place softened cream cheese in small bowl. Blend in sugar until light and fluffy. Spread in prepared pie shell. Arrange whole strawberries in prepared shell, standing on end and pressing into cream cheese. Set aside.

Place preserves in 2-cup measure. Microwave at High 1¼ to 2 minutes, or until hot and bubbly. Press through wire strainer into small bowl. Discard pulp. Spoon strained preserves over strawberries to glaze. Refrigerate at least 30 minutes before serving.

Pie à la Mode

Top one serving of pie with ice cream. Microwave at High 20 to 30 seconds, or until pie filling is warm to touch. For best results, ice cream should be frozen and pie at room temperature.

Cappuccino

Fill demitasse, coffee cup or mug half full of water. Microwave at High 1 to 3 minutes, or until boiling. Stir in instant espresso or coffee. Add enough milk to fill cup. Microwave 30 to 60 seconds, or until heated. Garnish with whipped cream, orange peel, dash ground nutmeg or dash ground cinnamon, if desired.

Lemon Sorbet

½ cup sugar
½ cup water
  Juice of 2 fresh lemons

Serves 4

In 2-cup measure or small bowl combine sugar and water. Microwave at High 1½ to 2 minutes, or until sugar is dissolved, stirring after half the time. Cool.

Add lemon juice to sugar water. Place in metal bowl. Freeze 6 to 8 hours, or until firm, stirring to break apart after half the time. Stir until smooth. Spoon into aperitif glasses or lemon cups. Serve between courses to refresh palate.

Frosted Glasses

Purée the sorbet about half an hour before serving. Spoon into stemmed glasses. Place in freezer 30 minutes. Handle glasses by stems to avoid marring the frost.

Cranberry-Orange Sorbet

½ cup sugar
½ cup water
  Juice of 2 fresh oranges
½ cup frozen whole cranberries or raspberries
2 tablespoons purchased or homemade Orange Liqueur, page 102
1 tablespoon frozen orange juice concentrate

Serves 4

In 2-cup measure or small bowl combine sugar and water. Microwave at High 1½ to 2 minutes, or until sugar is dissolved, stirring after half the time. Cool.

Stir fresh orange juice, frozen cranberries, liqueur and orange juice concentrate into sugar water. Pour into metal bowl. Freeze 6 to 8 hours, or until firm, stirring to break apart after half the time.

Place frozen mixture in food processor just before serving. Purée. Spoon into aperitif glasses. Serve between courses to refresh palate.

Peach Sorbet

½ cup sugar
½ cup water
1 cup sliced fresh or frozen peaches
2 tablespoons Raspberry Liqueur, page 103

Serves 4

In 2-cup measure or small bowl combine sugar and water. Microwave at High 1½ to 2 minutes, or until sugar is dissolved, stirring after half the time. Cool.

In metal bowl combine peaches and liqueur. Stir in sugar water. Freeze 6 to 8 hours, or until firm, stirring to break apart after half the time.

Place frozen mixture in food processor just before serving. Purée. Spoon into aperitif glasses. Serve between courses to refresh palate.

Plum Pudding

2 cups soft bread cubes
 (about 3 slices, trimmed)
½ cup all-purpose flour
½ cup currants
½ cup raisins
2 tablespoons packed dark
 brown sugar
½ teaspoon baking soda
½ teaspoon ground cinnamon
¼ teaspoon ground nutmeg
¼ teaspoon salt
¼ cup butter or margarine
½ cup half and half
2 tablespoons sherry
1 tablespoon plus 1½
 teaspoons molasses
1 egg
2 tablespoons brandy

Serves 4 to 6

Grease 2-cup measure. Cut two
1½-in. wide strips of wax paper
long enough to cover bottom
and sides of measure, with 1
inch of overhang on each side.
Overlap strips in base of
measure. Set aside.

Combine all ingredients except
brandy in medium bowl. Beat at
medium speed of electric mixer,
until well blended, scraping
bowl frequently. Pour batter into
prepared measure. Cover with
plastic wrap. Place in oven on
inverted saucer.

Microwave at 50% (Medium) 8
to 12 minutes, or until no
uncooked batter appears
through sides and cake feels
springy to the touch, rotating
every 2 minutes. Let stand,
covered, 5 minutes. Remove
plastic wrap. Loosen edges with
small spatula. Invert measure,
pulling wax paper strips to
remove pudding to serving
plate. To serve, place brandy in
small bowl. Microwave at High
about 20 seconds, or until
heated. Pour into large spoon or
ladle; ignite and spoon flaming
brandy over pudding.

Brandied Apricot Torte

1 pkg. (10¾ oz.) frozen loaf
    pound cake
1 cup apricot preserves
2 tablespoons brandy or
    homemade Apricot Brandy,
    page 103, divided
2 tablespoons butter or
    margarine
1 tablespoon light corn syrup
2 squares (2 oz.) semi-sweet
    baking chocolate

Serves 6

Trim crust, top and sides from pound cake. Cut lengthwise into thirds. Set aside. Place preserves in 2-cup measure. Microwave at High 1½ to 2 minutes, or until hot and bubbly. Press through wire strainer into small bowl. Discard pulp. Add 1 tablespoon brandy to strained liquid. Set aside.

To assemble cake, place bottom layer on wire rack. Spread with 2 tablespoons strained preserves. Add second layer and spread with 2 tablespoons strained preserves. Add top layer. Spread top and sides with remaining preserves. Refrigerate about 1 hour.

To prepare chocolate frosting, place butter, remaining 1 tablespoon brandy and the corn syrup in 2-cup measure. Microwave at High 1½ to 2 minutes, or until butter melts and mixture just comes to a boil. Add chocolate, stirring to melt. Cool until warm. Spread top and sides of cake with frosting. Refrigerate for about 30 minutes, or until frosting is firm. Transfer to serving plate.

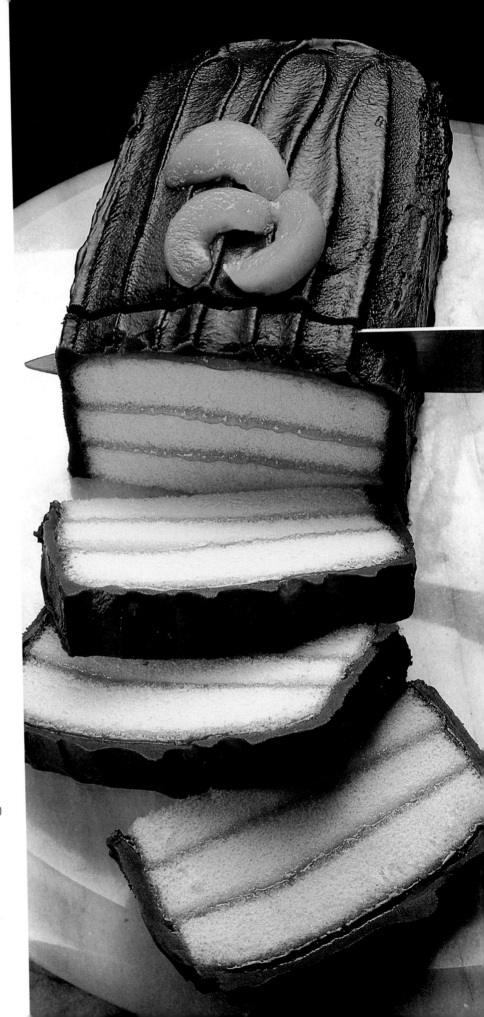

One-Dish Cooking

Explore the possibilities of one-dish cooking as a natural extension of microwaving's easy preparation and clean-up. Start with Short Rib Goulash, a traditional one-dish meal at microwave speed. Try the beautifully browned chicken, which makes it's own broth that you can use for soup. Microwave self-topping cakes. Just turn them out and serve; no frosting is needed. When you're cooking for one, microwave a timesaving meal-in-a-mug. For party fare, see pages 66 through 69, where one-dish microwaving goes elegant with vegetable assortments cooked and served on a single platter.

◄ Wine & Herb Stewed Chicken

2½ to 3-lb. whole broiler-fryer
   chicken
1 small onion, cut into 4
   wedges, divided
2 cloves garlic, peeled,
   divided
1 can (10½ oz.) condensed
   beef consommé
½ cup white wine
½ cup water
1 teaspoon dried rosemary
   leaves
1 teaspoon dried marjoram
   leaves
1 teaspoon salt
¼ teaspoon pepper
½ cup instant rice

Serves 4

Rinse chicken under cool running water. Pat dry. Place one onion wedge and one clove garlic inside cavity. Cut remaining garlic clove in half and rub on chicken skin. Discard cut garlic.

Place chicken in 3-qt. clay cooker or 4-qt. simmer pot. Add remaining three onion wedges. In 4-cup measure or small bowl mix remaining ingredients except rice. Pour over chicken. Cover. Microwave at High 35 to 45 minutes, or until meat near bone is no longer pink and juices run clear, rotating dish and basting chicken with broth 2 times. Add rice during last 5 minutes of cooking. Remove all the meat from the bones and strain the broth to make soup or carve and serve with buttered egg noodles.

Short Rib Goulash

2 lbs. beef short ribs
1 large onion, chopped
1 clove garlic, peeled and
   minced
1 teaspoon instant beef
   bouillon granules
1 cup water
1 can (28 oz.) whole tomatoes
3 small baking potatoes,
   peeled and cut lengthwise
   into 8 wedges
1 medium green pepper,
   seeded and cut into
   thin strips
1 cup thinly sliced carrots,
   ⅛-in. slices
¼ cup red wine
2 teaspoons packed brown
   sugar
1½ teaspoons paprika
½ teaspoon salt
½ teaspoon caraway seed
1 small dried hot red chili
   pepper, crushed

Serves 4 to 6

Combine short ribs, onion, garlic, bouillon granules and water in 3-qt. clay cooker or 4-qt. simmer pot. Cover. Microwave at High 10 minutes. Turn ribs over and rearrange. Re-cover. Reduce power to 50% (Medium). Microwave 40 to 50 minutes, or until meat is tender, rearranging and turning over 2 times. Remove ribs and cool. Remove meat from bones; discard fat and bones. Cut meat into small cubes. Skim fat from broth and discard. Return meat to broth.

Stir in tomatoes, potatoes, green pepper, carrots, wine, brown sugar, paprika, salt, caraway seed and chili pepper. Cover. Increase power to High. Microwave 5 minutes. Reduce power to 50% (Medium). Microwave 50 to 65 minutes, or until vegetables are tender, stirring 2 or 3 times. Let stand 10 minutes before serving.

Dessert in a Mug: Pudding

½ cup milk
½ square (1 oz.) semi-sweet
  baking chocolate
2 teaspoons cornstarch
1 tablespoon sugar
  Dash salt

Serves 1

Place milk and chocolate in
12-oz. microwave-safe mug or
2-cup measure. Microwave at
High 1 to 1½ minutes, or until
hot but not boiling. Stir to melt
chocolate. Combine cornstarch,
sugar and salt in small bowl.
Blend into milk and chocolate.
Microwave at High 30 to 45
seconds, or until mixture
thickens and just begins to boil,
stirring every 30 seconds. Watch
closely to prevent boilover.

Breakfast in a Mug: Scrambled Eggs

1 tablespoon butter or
  margarine, optional
1 or 2 eggs

1 tablespoon milk or water
  Dash salt
  Dash pepper

Serves 1

Place butter in 12-oz. microwave-safe mug or small bowl.
Microwave at High 30 to 45 seconds, or until melted. Add egg(s),
milk, salt and pepper. Stir or whip with fork. Microwave one egg at
High 35 to 45 seconds; two eggs 1¼ to 1¾ minutes, or until eggs
begin to set, stirring with fork to break apart after half the time.
Remove eggs when they are still soft and moist. Let stand about 2
minutes. Eggs will firm up while standing. If desired, sprinkle with
shredded cheese during standing time.

Bacon & Eggs

While eggs are standing, place one strip of bacon between paper
towels. Microwave 30 to 60 seconds. Crumble and add to eggs.

Lunch in a Mug: Soup

¾ cup non-fat dry milk powder
¼ cup non-dairy creamer
 2 tablespoons instant chicken
    bouillon granules
 1 tablespoon dried vegetable
    flakes
½ teaspoon dried parsley flakes
½ teaspoon dried summer
    savory

½ teaspoon salt
¼ teaspoon onion powder
¼ teaspoon pepper

To serve:
 2 tablespoons uncooked
    instant rice, optional
¾ cup water

Six ¾-cup servings

In small bowl combine dry milk powder, non-dairy creamer,
bouillon granules, vegetable flakes, parsley flakes, summer savory,
salt, onion powder and pepper. Store in airtight container no longer
than 6 months.

To make one serving of soup, place instant rice and 3 tablespoons
dry soup mix in microwave-safe mug. Place ¾ cup water in 1-cup
measure. Microwave at High 1½ to 3 minutes, or until boiling. Pour
into mug; stir. Cover with plastic wrap and let stand 5 minutes, or
until rice is tender.

Dinner in a Mug: Meat Loaf

¼ lb. lean ground beef
 1 slice white bread, torn into
    small pieces
 2 tablespoons milk
 1 green onion, thinly sliced
½ teaspoon Worcestershire
    sauce
¼ teaspoon seasoned salt
⅛ teaspoon pepper

Serves 1

Mix all ingredients thoroughly.
Press into 10-oz. microwave-
safe mug. Cover with wax
paper. Microwave at 70%
(Medium-High) 4 to 5½ minutes,
or until meat is firm, rotating
mug ½ turn after half the time.
Let stand 2 minutes.

Easy German Chocolate Cake

½ cup butter or margarine, divided
⅔ cup packed brown sugar, divided
⅔ cup flaked coconut, divided
⅔ cup finely chopped pecans, divided
1½ cups all-purpose flour
1⅓ cups granulated sugar
¼ cup cocoa
1½ teaspoons baking powder
1 teaspoon salt
1 cup milk
⅔ cup shortening
3 eggs
1 teaspoon vanilla

Makes 2-layer cake

Cut wax paper to fit bottoms of two 9-in. round cake dishes. Place ¼ cup butter in each lined dish. Microwave, one dish at a time, at High 45 seconds to 1¼ minutes, or until butter is melted and bubbly. Mix ⅓ cup brown sugar, ⅓ cup coconut and ⅓ cup pecans into butter in each dish. Spread into an even layer. Set dishes aside.

Place remaining ingredients in large bowl. Blend at low speed of electric mixer, scraping bowl constantly. Beat 2 minutes at medium speed, scraping bowl occasionally. Divide and spread batter into cake dishes.

Place one dish on inverted saucer in oven. Reduce power to 50% (Medium). Microwave 6 minutes, rotating ½ turn after half the time. Increase power to High. Microwave 2 to 4 minutes, or until cake is light and springy to the touch, rotating dish once. Sides will just begin to pull away from dish. Let stand directly on counter 5 minutes. Invert onto serving plate. Remove wax paper. Spread any topping from wax paper onto cake top. Repeat with remaining cake. Invert onto wire rack. Cool. Place second layer on top of first layer with frosting side up.

Caramel Apple-Topped Spice Cake

3 tablespoons butter or
    margarine
¼ cup packed dark brown
    sugar
1 medium cooking apple
1 cup all-purpose flour
⅔ cup granulated sugar
¾ teaspoon ground cinnamon
½ teaspoon baking soda
½ teaspoon salt
⅛ teaspoon ground nutmeg
⅓ cup shortening
⅓ cup buttermilk
2 eggs
½ teaspoon vanilla

Makes 9-in. cake

Cut wax paper to fit bottom of
9-in. round cake dish. Place
butter in 2-cup measure.
Microwave at High 30 to 45
seconds, or until melted. Stir in
brown sugar. Microwave at High
30 seconds, or until boiling. Stir
with fork until smooth. Spread
evenly in wax paper-lined dish.

Core and peel apple. Slice thinly.
Arrange five slices in center of
dish over caramel mixture.
Arrange remaining slices
around edge of dish, over-
lapping if necessary. Set aside.

Combine remaining ingredients
in large bowl. Blend at low
speed of electric mixer, scraping
bowl constantly. Beat 2 minutes
at medium speed, scraping
bowl occasionally. Spread
batter over apple slices. Place
dish on inverted saucer in oven.

Reduce power to 50% (Medium).
Microwave 6 minutes, rotating ½
turn after half the time. Increase
power to High. Microwave 2½
to 5½ minutes, or until cake is
light and springy to the touch,
rotating dish once. Let stand
directly on counter 5 minutes.
Invert onto serving plate.

Making Foods Look Good

Most meats and baked goods prepared in your microwave do not brown or form a crust. It is easy to make them more appetizing. The mixtures below will give a crust-like appearance or enhance eye appeal by adding color.

Cakes & Breads

To give microwaved cakes and breads a crust-like appearance and help retain freshness, lightly grease baking dish and sprinkle with one of the following crumb coatings.

Crumb Coatings	Crushed graham crackers, corn flake crumbs, crushed cookies, wheat germ, seasoned bread crumbs.

Sprinkle the top of quick breads, yeast breads or cakes with one of the following topping mixtures before microwaving. A brown surface is not necessary for layer cakes that will be frosted or topped with a dessert sauce.

Savory Topping	Mix together 2 tablespoons melted butter or margarine, ⅓ cup bread crumbs, 1 tablespoon Parmesan cheese and ½ teaspoon dried herbs.
Sweet Topping	Mix together 2 tablespoons melted butter or margarine, ⅓ cup graham cracker crumbs, 2 teaspoons sugar and 1 teaspoon ground cinnamon.
Streusel Topping	Mix together 2 tablespoons melted butter or margarine, ⅓ cup all-purpose flour, 3 tablespoons packed brown sugar, ¼ teaspoon ground cinnamon. (Add chopped pecans or shredded coconut, if desired.)

Pastry

Enhance the color and flavor of microwaved One-Crust Pastry, page 23, by substituting one of the following.

Whole Wheat Crust	Substitute ½ cup whole wheat flour for ½ cup all-purpose flour.
Light Wheat Crust	Add 2 tablespoons whole wheat flour.
Vanilla Crust	Blend 1 teaspoon vanilla into water.
Soy-Flavored Crust	Blend 1 teaspoon soy sauce into water.
Worcestershire-Flavored Crust	Blend 1 teaspoon Worcestershire sauce into water.
Cinnamon Crust	Blend 1 teaspoon ground cinnamon into flour before cutting in shortening.

Herb Mix

2 tablespoons instant beef
   bouillon granules
1 teaspoon dried bouquet
   garni seasoning
1 teaspoon dried parsley flakes
¼ teaspoon onion powder
¼ teaspoon pepper

Mix all ingredients. Store in
covered container.

Sprinkle desired amount on
poultry, beef or pork, rubbing
into meat before microwaving.

Barbecue Seasoning Mix

2 tablespoons paprika
¾ teaspoon ground coriander
¾ teaspoon chili powder
½ teaspoon celery seed
½ teaspoon ground nutmeg
½ teaspoon garlic salt
½ teaspoon pepper

Mix all ingredients. Store in
covered container. Sprinkle desired amount on poultry, beef or
pork, rubbing lightly into meat
before microwaving.

Peppery Ginger Mix

2 tablespoons instant beef
   bouillon granules
1 tablespoon coarse black
   pepper
½ teaspoon ground ginger

Mix all ingredients. Store in
covered container. Sprinkle desired amount on poultry, beef or
pork, rubbing lightly into meat
before microwaving.

Soy-Honey Baste ►

2 tablespoons butter or
   margarine
1 tablespoon honey
2 tablespoons soy sauce
¼ teaspoon dry mustard

Place butter in 1-cup measure.
Microwave at High 30 to 45
seconds, or until melted. Stir in
honey until dissolved.

Blend in remaining ingredients.
Brush on poultry, beef or pork
before and during microwaving.

Savory Baste ►

2 tablespoons butter or
   margarine
1 teaspoon dried parsley flakes
¼ teaspoon paprika
⅛ teaspoon poultry seasoning
¼ teaspoon bouquet sauce

Place butter in 1-cup measure.
Microwave at High 30 to 45
seconds, or until melted. Stir in
remaining ingredients. Brush
sauce on poultry before and
during microwaving.

Teriyaki Baste

1 tablespoon dark corn syrup
1 tablespoon teriyaki sauce
¼ teaspoon lemon pepper

Mix all ingredients in small bowl.
Brush or rub into poultry, beef
or pork before microwaving.
Brush remaining sauce on
during microwaving.

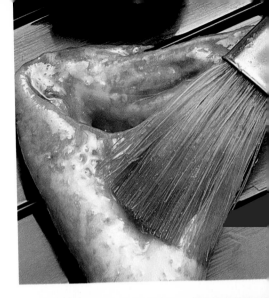

Meat

These glazes, like the seasoning mixes and bastes above, enhance the color of microwaved meats.

Molasses & Corn Syrup Glaze	Mix molasses and corn syrup in equal parts. Brush on ham or pork roast during microwaving.
Orange Marmalade, Currant Jelly or Apple Jelly Glaze	Microwave ½ cup jelly at High 1 to 1½ minutes, or until melted. Brush on ham, pork roast, chicken, turkey or duckling after half the cooking time.

Fruits, Peels & Nuts

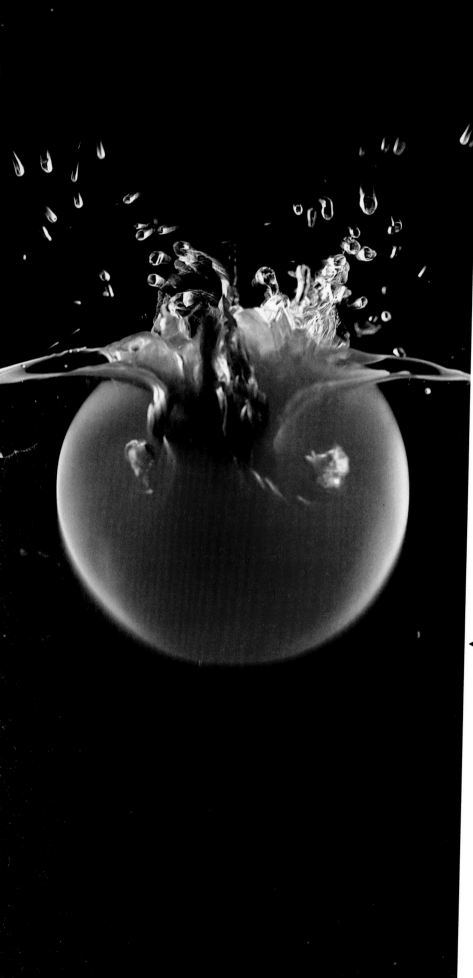

Fruits & Peels

The microwave oven cooks fresh or dried fruits quickly for true fruit taste, and also aids in everyday preparations like peeling and juicing. Use lemon and orange rinds to prepare your own extracts and dried or candied peels.

Airtight Jars

Save pimiento jars and spice bottles for microwave dried fruit peels and citrus extracts. Instant coffee or tea jars make good containers for candied peels.

◀ **Peel Tomatoes, Peaches, Nectarines & Apricots.** Place 4 cups water in large bowl or 3-qt. casserole. Cover with plastic wrap or glass lid. Microwave at High 8 to 11 minutes, or until boiling. Place three fruits in water. Let stand 1 to 1½ minutes. Remove fruit to bowl of cold water. Skin will then peel easily. Do only three pieces at a time. For additional fruit, return water to boiling and repeat procedure. For one or two fruits, place 1 cup water in small bowl or 2-cup measure. Microwave, covered, at High 2 to 3 minutes, or until boiling. Do only one piece at a time. Proceed as directed above.

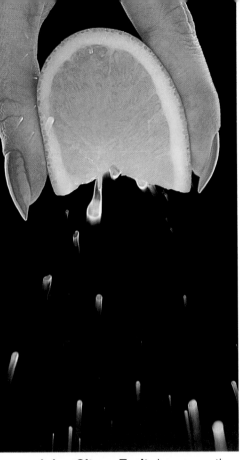

Juice Citrus Fruit. Increase the amount of juice from fresh oranges, grapefruit, lemons or limes. Before cutting and squeezing, microwave at High 20 to 35 seconds, or until slightly warm to the touch.

Plump Dried Fruit. Place 1 cup dried fruit (raisins, apricots, prunes or mixed dried fruit) in small bowl. Sprinkle with 1 table-spoon water. Cover with plastic wrap. Microwave at High 30 to 60 seconds, or until plumped and softened, stirring after half the time. Let stand, covered, 2 to 3 minutes. Drain any remaining liquid.

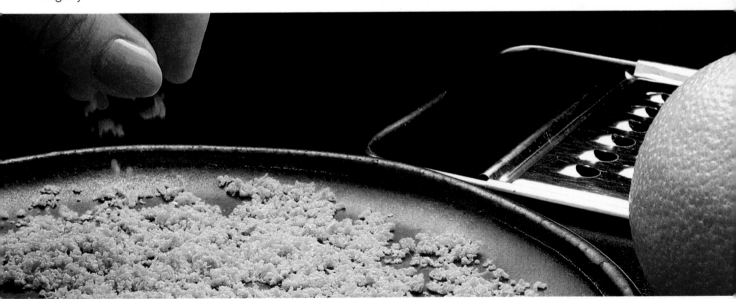

Dried Orange & Lemon Peel. Sprinkle grated peel from one medium orange or two small lemons (about 2 tablespoons) evenly in single layer on plate. Microwave at High 2 to 4 minutes, or until dry to the touch, turning plate and lifting and tossing peel with fingers after each minute. Let stand about 2 hours, or until completely cooled and brittle.

Store in small airtight container no longer than 2 months.

NOTE: ½ teaspoon dried peel is equivalent to 1 teaspoon grated fresh peel.

◄ Lemon or Orange Extract

1 lemon or orange
½ cup vodka

Makes ½ cup

Remove peel from lemon with vegetable peeler or zester. Do not include white membrane. Place peel in 4-oz. bottle. Add vodka. Microwave at High 30 to 45 seconds, or until bottle is warm to the touch. Cap bottle. Let stand at room temperature about 2 weeks before using.

Stewed Fruit

1 cup dried fruit (prunes, apricots, apples or mixed dried fruit)
½ cup water

Makes 1 cup

Place dried fruit in 1½-qt. casserole; sprinkle with water. Cover. Microwave at High 2 to 4 minutes, or until water boils, stirring after each minute. Let stand, covered, 5 minutes. Stir before serving. Sprinkle with cinnamon, if desired.

Candied Pineapple ▲

1 cup sugar
1 can (20 oz.) pineapple slices, packed in own juice, drained and ⅓ cup juice reserved
2 tablespoons light corn syrup
Sugar

Makes 10 slices

In 3-qt. casserole combine 1 cup sugar, ⅓ cup reserved pineapple juice and the corn syrup. Arrange five pineapple slices in single layer over sugar mixture. Microwave at High 8 to 12 minutes, or until sugar dissolves and slices are glossy and transparent on edges, turning over and rearranging every 4 minutes. Remove slices to wire rack to cool. They will become more transparent as they stand.

Add remaining slices to hot syrup. Microwave as directed above. Cool. When slices have cooled completely, coat with sugar. Cover with wax paper and let stand on wire rack at least 24 hours to dry. Re-coat with sugar. Slices will be slightly sticky. Store in airtight container with wax paper between layers no longer than 2 weeks.

Candied Peel

3 large oranges
1 lemon
6⅓ cups water, divided
⅔ cup granulated sugar
¼ cup powdered sugar

Makes 1 cup

How to Microwave Candied Peel

Remove peel from oranges and lemon with vegetable peeler or zester. Do not include the white membrane of the fruit.

Combine 2 cups water and the strips of peel in 4-cup measure or medium bowl. Microwave at High 4 to 6 minutes, or until water boils. Drain.

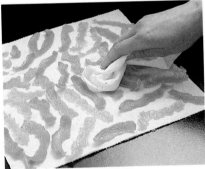

Repeat process 2 more times, boiling all the peel in 2 cups of water each time. Rinse peel. Drain on paper towels; pat dry.

Combine ⅓ cup water and the granulated sugar in 3-qt. casserole. Stir in peel. Microwave at High 6 to 8 minutes, or until sugar dissolves and peel is glossy and transparent, stirring every 2 minutes.

Remove peel with slotted spoon to rack. Cool. Sift powdered sugar over peel. Let cool completely. Store in airtight container no longer than 1 month.

Serve as a dipper for chocolate fondue, or add one strip of peel to cup of coffee or hot chocolate to flavor the drink.

Nuts & Seeds

Turn to your microwave oven whenever you need to shell or toast nuts for baking, garnishing or snacking. Even chestnuts and Brazil nuts shell easily after microwaving. Toasting nuts and seed enhances their flavor.

◄ **Shelled Nuts.** Shell nuts which are difficult to remove whole when cracked. In medium bowl or 2-qt. casserole combine 8 ounces of unshelled walnuts, pecans, Brazil nuts, filberts or almonds and 1 cup water. Cover with plastic wrap. Microwave at High 2½ to 4 minutes, or until water boils. Let stand 1 minute; drain. Spread on paper towels to cool. Crack shells and remove nutmeats. Shells will contain hot water, so open them carefully.

Peeled Chestnuts. Start with ¼ pound (about 1 cup) of nuts. Make a horizontal cut through shell of each chestnut without cutting nutmeat. Cut should extend across width of rounded side and just past edges of flat side. Place chestnuts in 4-cup measure or 1-qt. casserole. Pour in 1 cup water. Cover with plastic wrap or glass lid. Microwave at High 2½ to 4 minutes, or until water boils. Boil 1 minute. Let stand 5 to 10 minutes.

Remove nuts one at a time from water. Peel shell and inner skin. Spread on paper towel to cool. Set aside any which do not peel easily; boil again.

Blanched Almonds. Place 1 cup water in 1-qt. casserole; cover. Microwave at High 2 to 3½ minutes, or until boiling. Add 1 cup unblanched whole shelled almonds. Microwave, uncovered, at High 1 minute. Drain. Slip skins off. Spread on paper towels to dry.

Toasted Almonds. Place 1 tablespoon butter or margarine in 9-in. pie plate. Microwave at High 30 to 45 seconds, or until melted. Stir in ½ cup blanched whole almonds or ¼ cup slivered or sliced almonds, tossing to coat. Microwave at High 3 to 7 minutes (whole) or 3½ to 4½ minutes (slivered or sliced), or until light golden brown, stirring every 2 minutes. Let stand 5 minutes. Almonds will continue to toast after they are removed from oven. Use as a garnish for vegetables or main dishes.

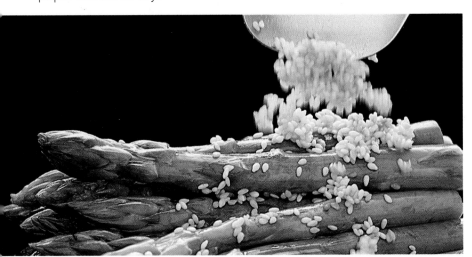

Toasted Sesame Seed. Place 1 tablespoon butter or margarine in 1-cup measure. Microwave at High 30 to 45 seconds, or until melted. Stir in 2 tablespoons sesame seed. Microwave at High 3 to 4½ minutes, or until light golden brown, stirring after each minute. Let stand 2 to 3 minutes. Seed will continue to toast after it is removed from oven. Drain seed on paper towel-lined plate. Sprinkle over cooked vegetables.

Toasted Coconut. Sprinkle ½ cup grated fresh coconut in thin layer in 9-in. pie plate. Microwave at 70% (Medium-High) 3 to 4 minutes, or until light brown, tossing with fork after each minute. Let cool. Store in airtight container no longer than 1 month. Serve with curry dishes or use as a dessert garnish.

Roasted Peanuts

1 cup shelled raw peanuts
1 teaspoon vegetable oil

Makes 1 cup

Place peanuts in 9-in. pie plate. Add oil, tossing to coat nuts. Microwave at High 5 to 7 minutes, or until barely light brown, stirring every 2 minutes. Peanuts may be browner on inside and will continue to roast after they are removed from oven. Cool on double thickness of paper towels. Salt, if desired.

Microwaved Nuts

Microwaved nuts heat quickly and brown evenly. Remove them from the oven as soon as they start to color; they brown as they stand.

Savory Snack Mix

3 cups thin pretzel sticks
1 cup Spanish peanuts
2 tablespoons butter or margarine

2 teaspoons Worcestershire sauce
½ teaspoon chili powder
⅛ teaspoon garlic salt
¼ teaspoon red pepper sauce

Makes 4 cups

In large bowl combine pretzels and peanuts. Set aside. In 1-cup measure combine butter, Worcestershire sauce, chili powder, garlic salt and red pepper sauce. Microwave at High 45 to 60 seconds, or until butter melts. Stir. Pour over pretzels and peanuts, tossing to coat. Microwave at High 3 to 5 minutes, or until mixture is hot and butter is absorbed, stirring after each minute. Spread on paper towels to cool.

Variation:
Substitute ½ cup cashews for ½ cup of the Spanish peanuts.

Orange-Spiced Pecan Brittle

½ cup granulated sugar
½ cup packed brown sugar
¼ cup dark corn syrup
 2 tablespoons water
¼ teaspoon salt
¼ teaspoon ground cinnamon
¼ teaspoon ground nutmeg

1 cup chopped pecans
1 tablespoon butter or
  margarine
1 teaspoon baking soda
½ teaspoon orange extract or
  homemade Orange
  Extract, page 88

Makes ¾ lb. or
2 cups crushed

Line large baking sheet with foil. In large bowl, combine granulated sugar, brown sugar, corn syrup, water, salt, cinnamon and nutmeg. Microwave at High 5 minutes. Stir in pecans. Insert microwave candy thermometer. Microwave at High 1½ to 4½ minutes, or until temperature is 300°F. (hard crack stage*), stirring after each minute.

Stir in butter, baking soda and orange extract until light and foamy. With rubber spatula, quickly spread to thin layer on prepared baking sheet. Cool. Break apart. Serve as a snack, or crush for use as a dessert topping. Store in airtight container no longer than 2 months.

*Hard Crack Stage: Syrup separates into hard, brittle threads when dropped into cold water.

Amaretto Glazed Almonds

 3 tablespoons Amaretto
½ cup blanched whole
  almonds, page 91

Makes ½ cup

Place Amaretto in 9-in. pie plate. Stir in almonds, tossing to coat. Microwave at High 4 to 5 minutes, or until glazed and light golden brown, stirring after each minute. Almonds will continue to toast after they are removed from oven. Spread on sheet of foil to cool. Store in airtight container. Serve as a snack or dessert garnish.

Homemade
Specialties

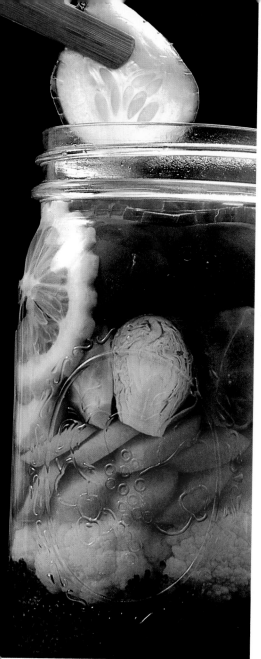

Pickles & Relishes

It's easy to microwave small batches of jellies, pickles and fruit syrups. Microwaving is cooler, cleaner, and faster than conventional methods, and small batches can provide more variety. These homemade specialties have true, natural flavor. They make welcome gifts when presented in an attractive bottle.

Pickles

These pickles are prepared in a quick pickling liquid, and are packed into sterilized jars after microwaving. They are not pressure- or water bath-canned so they require refrigeration.

◄ Antipasto Jar

Pickling Liquid:

1 cup water	1 tablespoon salt
½ cup Onion-Garlic Vinegar, page 100, or cider vinegar	1 tablespoon vegetable oil

Three cups fresh vegetables: Use a combination of the following to equal 3 cups:

Broccoli flowerets and stalks, sliced ¼ in. thick	Sliced carrots, ¼-in. thick
	Cauliflowerets
Brussels sprouts (¼ lb.), cut in half lengthwise	½ cup water

One cup fresh vegetables: Use a combination of the following to equal 1 cup:

Fresh whole mushrooms, 1-in. diameter	Green pepper, cut into 1-in. pieces
Green or ripe olives	Sliced cucumber

Garnish: Add one or more of the following:

1 lemon slice	1 sprig fresh dill, basil or oregano
1 bay leaf	

Follow photo directions, below.

Makes 1 quart

How to Microwave Antipasto Jar

Mix pickling liquid in 4-cup measure. Microwave at High 3½ to 5½ minutes, or until boiling, stirring after half the time.

Combine desired 3 cups vegetables in 2-qt. casserole. Add ½ cup water. Cover.

Microwave at High 2 to 4 minutes, or until color of vegetables intensifies, stirring once.

Pickled Carrots

12 oz. fresh tiny whole carrots
¼ cup water

Pickling Liquid:
½ cup cider vinegar
⅓ cup sugar
½ to 1 teaspoon salt
⅛ teaspoon celery seed
⅛ teaspoon mustard seed
⅛ teaspoon dried crushed red
    pepper
4 whole cloves
4 whole peppercorns
2 small cloves garlic, peeled
1 bay leaf
1 stick cinnamon

Makes 1 pint

Wash and scrub or peel carrots; trim ends. Place in 1½-qt. casserole. Add water; cover. Microwave at High 3 to 4 minutes, or until tender-crisp, stirring after half the time. Place under cold running water until cool. Drain. Pack into sterilized 1-pint jar or two ½-pint jars. Set aside.

In 2-cup measure combine pickling liquid ingredients. Microwave at High 1 to 2 minutes, or until boiling, stirring after half the time to dissolve the sugar and salt. Pour over carrots in the jar. Cover. Refrigerate 1 week before serving. Store in refrigerator no longer than 1 month.

Place immediately under cold running water until cool. Drain. Add remaining 1 cup vegetables.

Pack vegetables into sterilized 1-qt. jar, layering if desired. Include choice of garnish.

Pour pickling liquid over vegetables. Cover. Refrigerate 2 to 3 days before serving. Store in refrigerator no longer than 1 month.

Watermelon Pickles

1 lb. watermelon rind
½ cup sugar
½ cup cider vinegar
1 tablespoon chopped
  crystallized ginger
2 teaspoons grated fresh
  orange peel or 1 teaspoon
  Dried Orange Peel, page 87
4 whole cloves
1 stick cinnamon

Makes 1 pint

Trim dark green outer skin from rind. Cut trimmed rind into 1-in. chunks. (Yields 3 cups.) Place chunks in 1½-qt. casserole. Add sugar, tossing to coat. Cover and let stand overnight.

Stir in vinegar, ginger, orange peel and cloves. Add cinnamon. Microwave, uncovered, at High 10 to 13 minutes, or until chunks are transparent, stirring every 3 minutes. Remove cinnamon stick. Spoon into hot sterilized 1-pint jar; cover. Refrigerate 1 week before serving. Store in refrigerator no longer than 1 month.

Cabbage Relish

2½ cups shredded green or
  red cabbage
¾ cup chopped red onion
½ cup chopped green pepper
1 cup white vinegar
⅔ cup sugar
2 teaspoons salt
½ teaspoon celery seed
½ teaspoon mustard seed
¼ teaspoon ground turmeric

Makes 2 pints

In medium bowl combine cabbage, red onion and green pepper. Divide mixture equally between two sterilized 1-pint jars. Set aside.

In 4-cup measure combine vinegar, sugar, salt, celery seed, mustard seed and turmeric. Microwave at High 2 to 4 minutes, or until boiling, stirring after half the time to dissolve sugar and salt. Divide between the two jars; cover. Refrigerate 1 week before serving. Store in refrigerator no longer than 1 month.

Corn Relish

3 cups frozen whole kernel
  corn
½ cup chopped green pepper
¼ cup chopped onion
2 tablespoons chopped
  pimiento, drained
1 cup white vinegar
⅔ cup sugar
1 teaspoon salt
1 teaspoon celery seed
½ teaspoon mustard seed
½ to ¾ teaspoon red pepper
  sauce

Makes 2 pints

In medium bowl combine corn, green pepper, onion and pimiento. Microwave at High 1½ to 2½ minutes, or until corn is defrosted but cool to the touch, stirring after half the time. Divide equally between two sterilized 1-pint jars. Set aside.

In 4-cup measure combine remaining ingredients. Microwave at High 2 to 4 minutes, or until boiling, stirring after half the time to dissolve sugar and salt. Divide mixture between the two jars; cover. Refrigerate 1 week before serving. Store in refrigerator no longer than 1 month.

Apple-Pear Chutney

2 medium apples, cored and
    chopped
2 medium pears, peeled,
    cored and chopped
1½ cups packed dark brown
    sugar
1 cup cider vinegar
¾ cup chopped onion
⅔ cup chopped green pepper
½ cup chopped dates
1 tablespoon chopped
    crystallized ginger
1 teaspoon salt
1 teaspoon dry mustard
4 whole cloves
4 whole allspice
2 bay leaves
1 stick cinnamon

Makes 2 pints

Combine apples, pears, brown sugar, vinegar, onion and green pepper. Process in food processor, turning motor on and off 4 to 6 times, or place in blender and process 10 to 15 seconds, or until chopped but not puréed. (Process in two batches, if necessary.) Place mixture in 2-qt. casserole. Stir in remaining ingredients.

Microwave at High 18 to 25 minutes, or until very thick, stirring 3 or 4 times. Cool to room temperature. Discard bay leaves and cinnamon stick.

Divide equally between two sterilized 1-pint jars; cover. Refrigerate 1 week before serving. Store in refrigerator no longer than 1 month.

NOTE: Use as a condiment for meat or curry dishes.

Transform Leftovers

Save watermelon rind for Watermelon Pickles, opposite. Use leftover cabbage in Cabbage Relish, opposite. When you fix a selection of raw vegetables for a relish or appetizer tray, set some aside to make an Antipasto Jar, page 96, the next day.

◄ Onion-Garlic Vinegar

2 cloves garlic, peeled
2 pearl onions, peeled
  Wooden skewer, 6-in. long
1 or 2 cups white or cider
  vinegar

Makes 1 or 2 cups

Alternate garlic cloves and pearl onions on skewer. Drop into bottle. Add vinegar. Microwave, uncovered, at High 30 seconds to 1½ minutes, or until bottle is just warm to the touch; check every 30 seconds. Cap and let stand in a cool, dark place 2 weeks before using. After opening, store in refrigerator no longer than 2 months.

NOTE: Use in Marinated Vegetables or Garden Salad Dressing, opposite. Substitute for cider or white vinegar.

Herb Vinegar

1 sprig fresh mint, fresh
  tarragon, or fresh oregano
1 or 2 cups white or cider
  vinegar

Makes 1 or 2 cups

Place one or more sprig desired herb in bottle. Add vinegar. Microwave, uncovered, at High 30 seconds to 1½ minutes, or until bottle is just warm to the touch; check every 30 seconds. Cap and let stand in a cool, dark place 2 weeks before using. After opening, store in refrig-erator no longer than 2 months.

NOTE: Use Mint-Flavored Herb Vinegar in Fruit Salad Dressing, opposite. Substitute any of these Herb Vinegars for either white or cider vinegar.

Marinated Vegetables ▲

Marinade:
 ½ cup Onion-Garlic Vinegar,
    opposite
 ⅓ cup vegetable or olive oil
1½ teaspoons sugar
 1 teaspoon salt
 ½ teaspoon dried basil leaves
 ¼ teaspoon dry mustard
 ¼ teaspoon pepper

Vegetables:
 1 cup broccoli flowerets
 1 cup cauliflowerets
 1 cup sliced carrots
 2 tablespoons water
 8 oz. fresh whole mushrooms
 4 cherry tomatoes, cut into
    halves or 1 tomato, cut
    into wedges

Serves 4 to 6

In 1-cup measure or bowl blend
marinade ingredients. Set aside.

Combine broccoli flowerets,
cauliflowerets, carrots and water
in 2-qt. casserole; cover. Microwave at High 3 to 4 minutes, or
until colors become vibrant,
stirring after half the time. Drain.
Add mushrooms and tomatoes.
Stir marinade; pour over vegetables. Cover and refrigerate 3
to 4 hours before serving.

Fruit Salad Dressing ▶

 ¼ cup Mint-Flavored Herb
    Vinegar, opposite
 ½ cup vegetable oil
 1 tablespoon honey
 ⅛ teaspoon celery seed
 ½ teaspoon grated fresh orange
    peel or ¼ teaspoon Dried
    Orange Peel, page 87

Makes ¾ cup

Place all ingredients in jar or
shaker. Cover and shake until
mixed. Refrigerate no longer
than 1 week. Use as a dressing
for fresh fruit salad or lettuce.

Garden Salad Dressing

 ¼ cup Onion-Garlic Vinegar,
    opposite
 ½ cup vegetable oil
 ⅛ teaspoon celery seed
 ½ teaspoon dry mustard
 2 teaspoons Worcestershire
    sauce
 2 tablespoons grated
    Parmesan cheese

Makes ¾ cup

Place all ingredients in jar or
shaker. Cover and shake until
mixed. Refrigerate no longer
than 1 week. Use as a dressing
for tossed green salad.

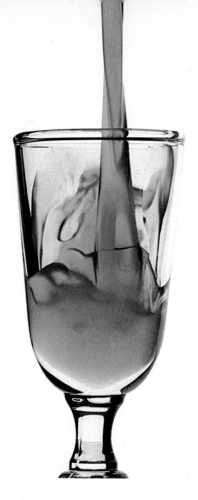

Orange Liqueur

3 oranges
1 cup sugar
1 stick cinnamon
2 cups brandy

Makes about 3 cups

Remove the peel from one orange with vegetable peeler or zester. Do not include white membrane. Cut oranges in half; squeeze juice. (Yields 1 cup.) In 4-cup measure combine orange peel, orange juice, sugar and cinnamon. Microwave at High 3 to 4 minutes, or until boiling, stirring after each minute. Boil 30 seconds. Watch closely; stir if necessary to prevent boilover. Cool to room temperature.

Remove cinnamon stick. Strain cooled juice mixture through cheesecloth. Add brandy to the strained liquid. Pour into bottle; cap. Let stand in a cool, dark place 1 month before serving. Shake bottle occasionally to mix.

Creme de Menthe

1½ cups sugar
1 cup water
1½ cups vodka or gin
1 teaspoon mint flavor
¼ teaspoon green food coloring

Makes about 4 cups

In 4-cup measure or large bowl combine sugar and water. Microwave at High 4 to 5 minutes, or until boiling. Boil 5 minutes. Watch closely; stir if necessary to prevent boilover.

Cool to room temperature. Skim any foam from top. Stir in remaining ingredients.

Pour into bottle; cap. Let stand in a cool, dark place 1 month before serving. Shake bottle occasionally to mix.

Anise Liqueur

1½ cups light corn syrup
½ cup water
¼ teaspoon instant unflavored, unsweetened tea powder
1½ cups vodka
¾ teaspoon anise extract
½ teaspoon vanilla
2 drops yellow food coloring

Makes 3½ cups

In 4-cup measure or large bowl combine corn syrup, water and tea powder. Microwave at High 4 to 5½ minutes, or until boiling. Watch closely; stir if necessary to prevent boilover. Cool to room temperature.

Skim any foam from top. Stir in vodka, anise extract, vanilla and yellow food coloring. Pour into bottle; cap. Let stand in a cool, dark place 1 month before serving. Shake bottle occasionally to mix.

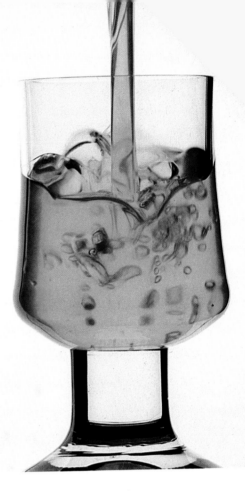

Raspberry Liqueur

2 pkgs. (10 oz. each) frozen
   raspberries in syrup
1½ cups sugar
1½ cups vodka

Makes 3 cups

Remove raspberries from
packages and place in large
bowl. Microwave at 50%
(Medium) 4 to 5 minutes, or
until partially defrosted. Gently
separate with fork. Let stand to
complete defrosting. Drain juice
into 8-cup measure or large
bowl. Set raspberries aside.

Add sugar to juice. Microwave
at High 3 to 5 minutes, or until
sugar dissolves and mixture
boils, stirring every 2 minutes.
Cool to room temperature. Skim
any foam from top. Add reserved
raspberries and vodka. Pour
into bottle; cap. Let stand in a
cool, dark place 1 month before
serving. Shake bottle occasionally
to mix. Strain through cheesecloth before serving. Serve
raspberries over ice cream.

Coffee Liqueur

1½ cups sugar
 1 cup water
 ¼ cup instant coffee crystals
1½ cups vodka
 1 vanilla bean or 1 teaspoon
   vanilla extract

Makes 2½ cups

In 4-cup measure or large bowl
combine sugar and water.
Microwave at High 4 to 5
minutes, or until boiling. Boil 5
minutes. Watch closely; stir if
necessary to prevent boilover.

Stir in coffee crystals until
dissolved. Cool to room temperature. Skim any foam from
top. Add vodka and vanilla bean.

Pour into bottle; cap. Let stand
in a cool, dark place 1 month
before serving. Shake bottle
occasionally to mix.

Apricot Brandy

1 pkg. (6 oz.) dried apricots
1½ cups white wine
 1 cup sugar
 1 cup brandy

Makes about 3 cups

If desired, chop apricots. In
4-cup measure combine
apricots, wine and sugar. Cover
with plastic wrap. Microwave at
High 4 to 6 minutes, or until
sugar dissolves and mixture
boils, stirring every 2 minutes.
Cool to room temperature. Skim
any foam from top. Add brandy.

Pour into bottle; cap. Let stand
in a cool, dark place 1 month
before serving. Shake bottle
occasionally to mix. Strain
through cheesecloth before
serving. Serve apricots over
ice cream.

Liqueurs

Serve liqueurs in Chocolate Liqueur Cups, page 54; stir into softened ice cream, page 58; or give as gifts.

Fruit Jelly ▲

1 can (6 oz.) frozen apple, grape, pineapple or tangerine juice concentrate
2 cups water

1 box (1¾ oz.) powdered fruit pectin
3½ cups sugar

Makes 2½ pints

In 3-qt. casserole or 8-cup measure combine juice concentrate and water. Stir in pectin until dissolved. Microwave at High 7 to 14 minutes, or until boiling, stirring every 3 minutes. Boil 1 minute. Gradually stir in sugar until blended.

Microwave at High 5 to 7 minutes, or until mixture returns to a boil, stirring carefully every 2 minutes to prevent boilover. Boil 1 minute. Skim any foam from top. Pour into hot sterilized ½-pint jars. Cover with hot sterilized lids and screw bands. Invert jar and quickly return to upright position. Or, if desired, seal jars with paraffin wax (see page 153). Store in a cool, dark place no longer than 6 months.

Variations:

Zesty Grape Jelly: Stir 1 teaspoon fresh lemon juice into Grape Jelly after skimming foam.

Mint Apple Jelly: Stir 5 to 7 drops green food coloring and 1 teaspoon mint extract into Apple Jelly after skimming foam.

◄ Wine Jelly

2¾ cups rosé wine, white wine or pink champagne
1 box (1¾ oz.) powdered fruit pectin

1 stick cinnamon
3 whole cloves
3½ cups sugar

Makes 2½ pints

In 3-qt. casserole or 8-cup measure combine wine, pectin, cinnamon stick and cloves. Microwave at High 5 to 10 minutes, or until boiling, stirring every 3 minutes. Boil 1 minute. Gradually stir in sugar until blended.

Microwave at High 3 to 6½ minutes, or until mixture returns to a boil, stirring carefully every 2 minutes to prevent boilover. Boil 1 minute. Skim any foam from top. Pour into hot sterilized ½-pint jars, or glasses. Cover with hot sterilized lids and screw bands. Invert jar and quickly return to upright position. Or, if desired, seal jars with paraffin wax (see page 153). Store in a cool, dark place no longer than 6 months.

Jellies

Microwaving small quantities of jelly from fruit concentrate is cool, clean and quick. While you're microwaving the jelly, sterilize jars conventionally or in your dishwasher.

Layered Jellies

Jellies can be layered in wine glasses, coffee mugs, or creamers as well as pint jars and jelly glasses. Sterilize the containers before use.

Choose jellies which have attractive color contrast and good flavor combination, such as Apple, Mint Apple and Grape, opposite.

Try Pineapple and Tangerine with a middle layer of Rosé or White Wine Jelly. For variety, suspend a piece of Candied Pineapple, page 88, or a maraschino cherry in the layer of Wine Jelly. Three batches of jelly yield 7½ pints.

How to Prepare Layered Jellies

Fill each jelly glass or other container one-third full. The first layer must begin to set before the next layer is added.

Prepare second layer. When first layer is sufficiently set, carefully spoon second layer into jar. Allow to set slightly.

Add final layer, carefully spooning over second layer. Top with paraffin wax (see page 153).

Fruit Syrups

Small batches of syrup can be microwaved using fresh or frozen fruit. Compare their true fruit flavor with commercial products; you'll agree they're worth the few minutes it takes to microwave them.

Fruit Syrups

1 bag (16 oz.) frozen raspberries, blackberries or blueberries
1 cup sugar
¾ cup light corn syrup

Makes 1 pint

How to Microwave Fruit Syrups

Place frozen fruit in medium bowl or 4-cup measure. Cover with plastic wrap. Microwave at High 6½ to 10 minutes, or until boiling, stirring every 3 minutes.

Line strainer with cheesecloth; place in 8-cup measure or 3-qt. casserole. Pour hot fruit into lined strainer.

Mash fruit with the back of spoon to press juice through strainer. (Yields about ½ to ¾ cup juice.) Discard pulp.

Add sugar and corn syrup to strained juice. Microwave at High 3 to 6 minutes, or until boiling, stirring every 2 minutes.

Boil 1 minute. Skim any foam from top. Pour syrup into hot sterilized 1-pint jar or catsup bottle; cap.

Refrigerate or store in a cool, dark place no longer than 6 months. Serve over pancakes, waffles or desserts.

Fresh Strawberry Syrup ▲

1 pint fresh strawberries, hulled
1 cup sugar
¾ cup light corn syrup

Makes 1 pint

Cut strawberries in half. Place in large bowl. Mash with fork. Cover. Microwave at High 4 to 5 minutes, or until boiling, stirring every 2 minutes. Line strainer with cheesecloth; place in 3-qt. casserole or 8-cup measure. Pour hot fruit into lined strainer. Mash fruit with the back of spoon to press juice through strainer. (Yields ½ to ¾ cup juice.) Discard pulp.

Add sugar and corn syrup to strained juice. Microwave at High 3 to 6 minutes, or until boiling, stirring every 2 minutes. Boil 1 minute. Skim any foam from top. Pour syrup into hot sterilized 1-pint jar or catsup bottle; cap. Refrigerate or store in a cool, dark place no longer than 6 months. Serve over pancakes, waffles or desserts.

Heat Syrup for Serving

Remove cap from bottle or jar. Microwave at High 30 to 60 seconds, or until bottle is warm to the touch.

Fresh Plum Syrup ▶

1 lb. very ripe purple plums
1 cup sugar
¾ cup light corn syrup

Makes 1 pint

Cut plums in half; remove pits. Cut halves into small pieces. Place in large bowl; cover. Microwave at High 5 to 8 minutes, or until plums cook down and mash easily, stirring every 2 minutes.

Line strainer with cheesecloth; place in 3-qt. casserole or 8-cup measure. Pour hot fruit into lined strainer. Mash fruit with the back of spoon to press juice through strainer. (Yields ½ to ¾ cup juice.) Discard pulp.

Add sugar and corn syrup to strained juice. Microwave at High 3 to 6 minutes, or until boiling, stirring every 2 minutes. Boil 1 minute. Skim any foam from top.

Pour syrup into hot sterilized 1-pint jar or catsup bottle; cap. Refrigerate or store in a cool, dark place no longer than 6 months. Serve over pancakes, waffles or desserts.

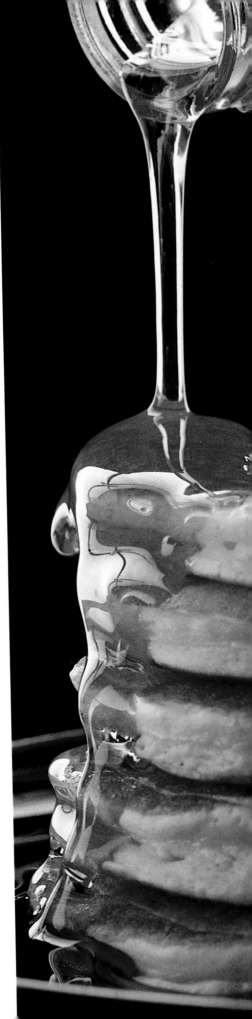

Just For Fun

Snacks

For many, a relaxing break in work or play calls for a snack. The ideal snack is one which is quick and easy to prepare. Use your microwave oven for snacks you can make ahead and keep on hand, and for almost-instant snacks you can produce on the spur of the moment.

Refresh & Rewarm Cookies

Place two cookies on napkin or paper towel. Microwave at High 15 to 30 seconds, or until warm to the touch.

Milk Shake ▲

3 scoops vanilla, chocolate or
   chocolate chip ice cream
2 tablespoons milk
2 tablespoons bottled
   chocolate syrup or
   Chocolate Syrup, right

Serves 1

Place all ingredients in 12-oz. glass. Microwave at 50% (Medium) 30 to 45 seconds, or until stirrable. If additional softening is needed, continue to microwave, stirring every 15 seconds, until of desired consistency.

Chocolate Syrup

⅓ cup instant chocolate-
   flavored drink mix
¼ cup light or dark corn syrup
2 tablespoons water

Makes ½ cup

In 4-cup measure combine drink mix, corn syrup and water. Microwave at High 45 seconds to 1½ minutes, or until boiling. Boil 1 minute, watching closely to avoid boilover. Cool and refrigerate. Mixture thickens as it cools. Store in jar in refrigerator no longer than 1 month.

Serve over ice cream or use in Milk Shake or Hot Cocoa, right.

Hot Cocoa

¾ cup milk
2 tablespoons bottled
   chocolate syrup or
   Chocolate Syrup, left

Serves 1

Place milk in microwave-safe mug. Blend in chocolate syrup. Microwave at High 1¼ to 2¼ minutes, or until hot (170°F.).

If desired, top hot cocoa with marshmallows, ice cream, miniature chocolate chips or whipped topping.

Nachos

24 large tortilla chips
 1 cup shredded Monterey
     Jack, Cheddar or Colby
     cheese
¼ teaspoon chili powder
⅛ teaspoon ground cumin

Serves 4

Arrange tortilla chips on 10-in.
plate or serving dish, or in 9-in.
cake dish. Place cheese in
plastic bag. Add chili powder
and cumin, shaking to coat.
Sprinkle over chips. Microwave
at 50% (Medium) 2 to 5
minutes, or until cheese melts,
rotating dish 1 or 2 times.

Variations:
Nachos With Beans: Spread
tortilla chips with refried beans.
Arrange on plate as directed
and sprinkle with cheese
mixture. Top with 2 tablespoons
chopped onion and 2 tablespoons sliced black or green
olives. Microwave as directed.
Sprinkle with chopped tomato,
shredded lettuce and taco
sauce before serving, if desired.

Nachos With Salsa: Place a
custard cup or small bowl in
center of 9-in. cake dish or
serving plate. Arrange tortilla
chips around edge. Sprinkle
with cheese mixture as directed.
Place ⅓ cup of salsa or taco
sauce in custard cup.
Microwave as directed.

Chilito

 1 flour tortilla, 8-in. diameter
½ cup shredded Colby,
     Cheddar or Monterey Jack
     cheese
 1 tablespoon chopped fresh or
     canned green chilies

Serves 1

Place tortilla on plate. Sprinkle
with cheese and chilies.
Microwave at 50% (Medium) 1
to 1½ minutes, or until cheese
melts, rotating after half the
time. Roll up.

Granola

3 cups old-fashioned rolled
  oats
½ cup shredded coconut
⅓ cup sliced almonds,
  chopped
⅔ cup honey
¼ cup packed dark brown
  sugar
¼ cup vegetable oil
1 teaspoon ground cinnamon
1 teaspoon vanilla
1 teaspoon molasses
½ cup raisins
⅓ cup chopped dried apples

Makes 6 cups

Granola Bars

6 cups Granola, left
½ cup butter or margarine
½ cup packed dark brown
  sugar

⅛ teaspoon salt
2 eggs, slightly beaten
¼ teaspoon almond extract

Makes 12 bars

Prepare granola as directed, except omit raisins. Set aside. Place butter in 2-cup measure or medium bowl. Microwave at High 45 seconds to 1½ minutes, or until melted. In medium bowl combine brown sugar, salt, eggs and almond extract. Beat in butter until combined. Stir in granola until coated. Press into greased 12 × 8-in. baking dish.

Microwave at High 6 to 9 minutes, or until firm to the touch, rotating dish ½ turn and pressing mixture with spatula every 2 minutes. Cut into twelve 4 × 2-in. bars. Cool completely before removing from dish. Store in refrigerator no longer than 1 week.

How to Microwave Granola

Mix rolled oats, shredded coconut and chopped almonds in large bowl. Set aside.

Combine remaining ingredients except raisins and apples in 8-cup measure. Microwave at High 2 to 3 minutes, or until boiling, stirring after each minute.

Pour honey mixture over oats, tossing to coat. Microwave at High 4½ to 7 minutes, or until mixture begins to stiffen and appear dry, stirring every 2 minutes. For crisper cereal, microwave 30 to 60 seconds longer, or until coconut begins to brown lightly.

Stir in raisins and apples. Allow mixture to cool about 1 to 1½ hours, stirring to break apart 1 or 2 times during cooling.

Popcorn

Popping corn in the microwave is fast and easy and requires little clean-up. Because it uses little or no oil, microwave popcorn is a light snack.

Fresh popcorn is low in moisture. To get the best yield of popped kernels, maintain low moisture by storing in an airtight jar in a dry, cool place.

Microwave popcorn poppers are essential equipment. Do not try to microwave popcorn in a brown paper bag; it could catch on fire. For amounts of popcorn and cooking times, follow the instructions for your popper. Don't overcook. Listen; corn is done as soon as it stops popping. Discard any unpopped kernels.

The popcorn snacks on these pages can be made with corn you pop yourself, or from bagged popped corn purchased from the supermarket. Leftover or purchased popcorn can also be rewarmed and refreshed in the microwave oven.

Cheese Popcorn ▲

 8 cups popped popcorn
¼ cup plus 2 tablespoons
　　butter or margarine
¼ cup grated American cheese
　　food

¼ cup grated Parmesan
　　cheese
Seasoned salt

Makes 8 cups

Place popcorn in large bowl. Set aside. Place butter in 2-cup measure. Microwave at High 45 seconds to 1¼ minutes, or until melted and bubbly. Stir in cheeses. Drizzle over popcorn. Toss to coat. Sprinkle with seasoned salt to taste.

Variation:
Substitute ¼ cup grated Romano cheese for the grated American cheese food.

Rewarm Popped Popcorn

Place 4 to 8 cups in large bowl. Microwave at High 45 seconds to 1½ minutes, or until popcorn is warm to the touch, tossing every 30 seconds. Do not overheat.

Caramel Corn

3 tablespoons butter or
    margarine
¾ cup packed brown sugar
⅓ cup shelled raw peanuts
3 tablespoons dark corn syrup
½ teaspoon vanilla
¼ teaspoon baking soda
    Dash salt
5 cups popped popcorn

            Makes 5 cups

NOTE: Soft Crack Stage: Syrup
separates into hard but not
brittle threads when dropped
into cold water.

How to Microwave Caramel Corn

Place butter in 8-cup measure
or large bowl. Microwave at High
30 to 45 seconds, or until melted.

Stir in brown sugar, peanuts
and corn syrup. Insert microwave candy thermometer.

Microwave at High 3 to 4
minutes, or until mixture reaches
280°F. (soft crack stage).

Mix in vanilla, baking soda and
salt. Place prepared popcorn in
large bowl.

Pour hot mixture quickly over
popcorn, stirring to coat. Microwave popcorn at High 2 minutes, stirring after half the time.

Stir again. Cool about 30
minutes, stirring occasionally to
break apart.

Hot Mustard Sauce

2 tablespoons dry mustard
3 tablespoons white wine or
    white wine vinegar
1 egg, slightly beaten
¼ cup sugar
    Dash salt

Makes ½ cup

In small bowl combine mustard
and wine. Let stand 1 hour.
Blend in egg, sugar and salt.
Microwave at 50% (Medium) 2
to 3 minutes, or until sauce
thickens and coats spoon,
stirring after each minute. Stir
before serving. Serve hot or
cold with Wonton Chips, below,
ham or egg rolls. Store in refrigerator no longer than 1 week.

Wonton Chips With Sauce

Hot Mustard Sauce, above,
    or Plum Sauce, below
3 wonton skins (4 × 4-in. each),
    cut diagonally into quarters

Serves 4

Prepare Hot Mustard Sauce or
Plum Sauce; set aside. Arrange
wonton pieces on outer edge of
serving dish. Microwave at High
1½ to 2½ minutes, or until light
brown (check underside),
rotating dish every 30 seconds.
Serve with prepared sauces.

Plum Sauce

2 teaspoons cornstarch
2 teaspoons soy sauce
½ cup Fresh Plum Syrup,
    page 107, or melted Plum
    Jelly, page 56
¼ cup white vinegar

Makes ⅔ cup

In 2-cup measure mix cornstarch and soy sauce. Blend in
Plum Syrup and vinegar.
Microwave at High 1 to 2
minutes, or until clear and
thickened, stirring every 30
seconds. Serve hot or cold with
Wonton Chips, above, ham or
egg rolls. Store in refrigerator no
longer than 1 week.

Stuffed Potato Shells

2 baking potatoes (5 to 7 oz. each)
1 slice bacon or 1 tablespoon prepared bacon bits
¼ teaspoon salt
⅛ teaspoon pepper
¼ cup dairy sour cream or dairy sour cream with chives
½ cup shredded Cheddar cheese
1 tablespoon sliced green onion

Serves 4

NOTE: Reserve the scooped out centers for mashed potatoes.

How to Microwave Stuffed Potato Shells

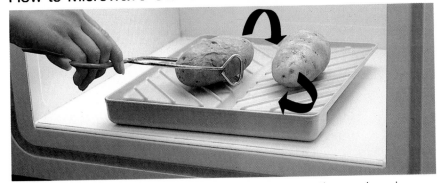

Scrub potatoes; pierce with fork. Arrange on roasting rack or in microwave muffin cups (see page 140). Microwave at High 5 to 7½ minutes, or until soft to the touch, rearranging and turning over after half the time. Let stand 5 minutes to complete cooking.

Place bacon slice between paper towels. Microwave at High 30 to 60 seconds, or until crisp. Crumble and set aside.

Slice each potato lengthwise in half, then crosswise. Carefully scoop out centers, leaving ¼ inch of potato next to skin. Arrange skins on serving plate.

Sprinkle with salt and pepper. Spread thin layer of sour cream in each shell. Sprinkle with cheese, green onion and crumbled bacon.

Microwave at 50% (Medium) 2½ to 4 minutes, or until cheese melts, rotating plate after half the cooking time.

Kids' Stuff

Create imaginative treats for children, like cake microwaved in a cone or a gingerbread house. Parents cook these recipes, but children participate.

Lollipops ▶

1 cup sugar
½ cup light corn syrup
¼ cup water
¼ teaspoon orange, lemon or peppermint extract
   Food coloring (orange, yellow or red), page 153
12 wooden popsicle sticks or lollipop sticks

Makes 12 lollipops

NOTE: Hard Crack Stage: Syrup separates into hard, brittle threads when dropped into cold water.

How to Microwave Lollipops

Mix sugar, corn syrup and water in 8-cup measure. Use wet pastry brush to wash sugar crystals from sides of measure. Insert microwave candy thermometer.

Microwave at High 9 to 12½ minutes, or until mixture reaches 310°F. (hard crack stage), stirring every 2 minutes. Stir in desired extract and food coloring.

Pour over sticks arranged on buttered foil, or pour into lollipop molds, below. Let stand about 1 hour, or until hard. Wrap in plastic wrap. Store in a cool, dry place.

How to Make Lollipop Molds

Cut 1 inch off top of twelve 9-oz. wax-coated paper drinking cups.

Grease inside of top portion of cup. Punch small hole in side of mold; insert stick.

Place molds on buttered foil. Fill as directed, above.

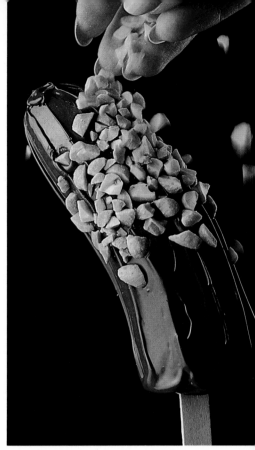

Butterscotch Crunch Bars

1 cup butterscotch chips
½ cup sugar
½ cup light corn syrup
½ cup peanut butter
4 cups corn flakes
½ cup chocolate chips

Makes 10 bars

In large bowl combine butterscotch chips, sugar, corn syrup and peanut butter. Microwave at High 1 to 1½ minutes, or until mixture can be stirred smooth. Stir in cereal.

Press into lightly greased 10 × 6-in. baking dish. Place chocolate chips in 2-cup measure or small bowl. Microwave at 50% (Medium) 1½ to 2 minutes, or until chips are glossy and can be stirred smooth. Spread melted chips on bars. Cool before cutting.

Fruit-Flavored Crispy Bars

⅓ cup butter or margarine
¼ cup fruit-flavored gelatin
    (half of 3-oz. pkg.)
1 pkg. (10½ oz.) marshmallows
8 cups crisp rice cereal

Makes 24 bars

Grease 12 × 8-in. baking dish. Place ⅓ cup butter in large bowl. Microwave at High 45 to 60 seconds, or until melted. Mix in gelatin. Stir in marshmallows, tossing to coat.

Microwave at High 1½ to 2 minutes, or until marshmallows melt, stirring after half the time. Immediately stir in cereal until well coated. Press into prepared dish with back of lightly buttered large spoon. Cool. Cut into 2-in. squares.

Remaining Gelatin

Microwave ½ cup water at High 1 to 2 minutes, or until boiling. Stir in gelatin until dissolved. Stir in ½ cup cold water. Chill. Serves 2.

Chocolate-Covered Bananas

3 large firm bananas
6 wooden popsicle sticks
1 cup semi-sweet chocolate
    chips
2 tablespoons shortening
½ cup chopped peanuts

Serves 6

Peel bananas; cut each in half crosswise. Insert wooden sticks. Place on wax paper-lined plate or baking sheet. Place chocolate chips and shortening in 2-cup measure. Microwave at 50% (Medium) 2½ to 4 minutes, or until chips are glossy and can be stirred smooth.

Spoon melted chocolate over each banana to coat. Allow any excess to drip back into bowl. Sprinkle bananas with peanuts. Place on wax paper-lined plate. Freeze until firm. Wrap in wax paper, label and freeze no longer than 2 weeks.

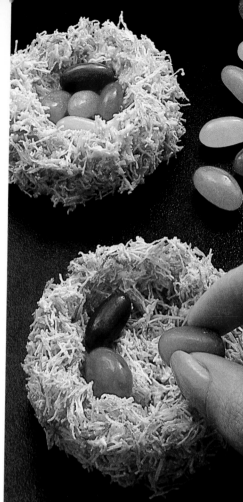

Graham Cracker Cookies

1 cup all-purpose flour
½ cup whole wheat flour
2 tablespoons sugar
½ teaspoon baking soda
¼ teaspoon salt
¼ teaspoon ground cinnamon
¼ cup shortening

1 tablespoon butter or
  margarine
2 tablespoons plus 1
  teaspoon water
1 tablespoon honey
1 tablespoon molasses
½ teaspoon vanilla

Makes 3 to 3½ dozen cookies

In medium bowl combine flours, sugar, baking soda, salt and cinnamon. Cut in shortening and butter until particles resemble small peas. In small bowl combine water, honey, molasses and vanilla. Sprinkle over dry mixture, tossing with fork until particles cling together and resemble small peas. Form into a ball. Cover with plastic wrap. Refrigerate at least 1 hour.

Divide dough in half. Roll out half the dough to ⅛-in. thickness between two sheets of wax paper. Cut with cookie cutters. Prick with fork. Line 10-in. plate with wax paper. Arrange 12 cookies around edge of plate. Microwave at High 1 to 2 minutes, or until dry and firm to the touch, rotating every 30 seconds. Cool on wire rack. Cookies will crisp as they cool. Repeat with remaining dough. Store in airtight container.

Edible Ornaments

1 tablespoon butter or
  margarine
1 cup miniature marshmallows
3 shredded wheat biscuits,
  crushed
  Jelly beans, red hot candies
  or black gumdrops, optional

Makes 4 to 6 ornaments

Place butter in medium bowl. Microwave at High 30 to 45 seconds, or until melted. Add marshmallows, stirring to coat. Microwave at High 30 to 60 seconds, or until marshmallows puff and mixture can be stirred smooth. Stir in crushed cereal.

Shape into Easter nests and fill with colored jelly beans; or shape into Christmas wreaths and decorate with red hot candies or melted candy coating, opposite; or shape into snowmen and decorate with black gumdrops and red hot candies.

Choose the Right Pouch

Be sure to use a heat-sealable, boilable pouch when melting candy coating. Do not use ordinary food storage or freezer bags; they are not designed to withstand the high temperature.

Candy Coating Ornaments

¼ lb. chocolate or white candy
    coating
1 heat-sealable pouch, 1-qt. size
Coloring book, optional

    Makes about 10 ornaments

How to Microwave Candy Coating Ornaments

Break candy coating into pieces. Place in heat-sealable pouch. Do not seal pouch.

Microwave at 50% (Medium) 3 to 4 minutes, or until soft to the touch. (Candy should be warm, not hot.)

Squeeze softened candy coating into one corner of pouch. Snip corner with scissors to form writing tip.

Draw designs with candy coating onto wax paper, or trace designs onto wax paper over coloring book for pattern ideas.

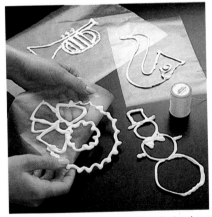

Let stand until firm. Peel design off wax paper. Place thread through ornaments for hanging.

Decorate ornaments while still soft. Use red hot candies, chocolate shot or miniature marshmallows, if desired.

Cake Decorations. Decorate cakes with candy coating (see Candy Coating Ornaments, page 121.) Write messages or draw designs with the coating.

Chocolate Fluff & Stuff ▲

¾ cup water
2 envelopes unflavored gelatin
⅔ cup sugar
¼ cup cocoa

½ cup milk
½ teaspoon vanilla
2 cups frozen whipped dessert topping, defrosted

Makes 8 × 8-in. dish

Place water in 1-cup measure; cover. Microwave at High 2 to 2½ minutes, or until boiling. Add gelatin; stir to dissolve. Set aside.

In small bowl combine sugar and cocoa. Slowly blend in milk, stirring to dissolve sugar and cocoa. Stir in vanilla. Blend in dissolved gelatin. Skim off any foam. Pour ½ cup of chocolate-gelatin mixture into small bowl. Blend in whipped topping. Pour remaining gelatin mixture into 8 × 8-in. baking dish. Spoon chocolate whipped topping mixture over and spread evenly with spatula. Refrigerate until firm, about 1 hour. Cut into 16 squares.

Fruit Squares

1½ cups water
3 envelopes unflavored gelatin

1 can (12 oz.) frozen grape juice concentrate

Makes 8 × 8-in. dish

Place water in 4-cup measure; cover. Microwave at High 3 to 5 minutes, or until boiling. Add gelatin; stir to dissolve. Add grape juice concentrate. Pour mixture into 8 × 8-in. baking dish. Refrigerate until firm, about 1 hour. Cut into bite-size pieces.

Domino Cake. Use white candy coating to decorate frosted chocolate cake or brownies to represent dominos.

Rocky Road Fudge Pops

1 pkg. (3⅝ oz.) chocolate
    pudding mix
2½ cups milk
  ½ cup marshmallow creme
  ⅓ cup chopped peanuts
  ¼ cup chopped chocolate
    chips
  6 wax-coated paper cups
    (9-oz. size)
  6 wooden popsicle sticks

Serves 6

How to Microwave Rocky Road Fudge Pops

Combine pudding mix and milk in 4-cup measure. Microwave at High 5½ to 6 minutes, or until slightly thickened, stirring every 2 minutes.

Cool pudding to room temperature. Fold in marshmallow creme to create "marbled" appearance. Set aside.

Mix chopped peanuts and chopped chocolate chips in small bowl. Spoon 1 heaping tablespoon of peanut mixture into each of six cups.

Add 1 tablespoon of pudding mixture to each cup and stir lightly to combine.

Divide remaining pudding mixture evenly between cups. Insert popsicle stick in center of each cup.

Freeze about 4 hours, or until firm. To serve, peel cups from frozen pops.

123

◀ **Cake Cones.** To prepare one cake cone, spoon about 2 tablespoons of prepared cake mix batter or muffin mix batter into flat-bottomed ice cream cone. Microwave at High 20 to 40 seconds, or until cake is light and springy to the touch. Some moist spots may remain, but will dry upon standing. Cool on wire rack. Let stand 3 minutes. Top with prepared whipped topping, frosting or scoop of ice cream, if desired.

For six cake cones, assemble as directed, above. Arrange in circle in oven. Microwave at High 1½ to 3 minutes, or until cake is light and springy to the touch, rearranging cones after half the time. Let stand 3 minutes and decorate.

Versatile Gingerbread

Microwave gingerbread to suit your taste. It can have a cake-like consistency, as directed for the gingerbread house, or cookie-crisp consistency. Make a gingerbread house from half of the dough. Cut remaining dough into cookies with decorative cutters. Microwave, six at a time, as directed for gingerbread house, opposite, or until firm to the touch. Cool on wire rack.

Gingerbread House

2½ cups all-purpose flour
½ teaspoon baking soda
½ teaspoon ground ginger
½ teaspoon ground cinnamon
¼ cup granulated sugar
¼ cup shortening
1 egg
½ cup molasses
1 square (1 oz.) semi-sweet baking chocolate, melted, page 50
1 cup powdered sugar
1 tablespoon water
Food coloring

Makes 2 gingerbread houses

How to Microwave a Gingerbread House

Combine flour, baking soda, ginger and cinnamon in medium bowl. In another bowl mix granulated sugar and shortening. Stir in egg, molasses and melted chocolate.

Add flour mixture to molasses mixture in three parts, stirring until combined. Knead in any remaining flour which cannot be stirred in. Divide dough in half; shape into two balls and flatten.

Wrap balls in plastic wrap. Refrigerate 2 hours. Roll one ball between wax paper to ⅛-in. thickness. Remove top piece of wax paper. Trim dough edges to make 8 × 8-in. square.

Score gingerbread into a house shape with serrated knife. Transfer on wax paper to cardboard. Microwave at 50% (Medium) 3½ to 6 minutes, or until firm to touch and no longer doughy, rotating every 2 minutes.

Cool on wire rack. Separate at perforations. Cool completely. With remaining dough make second house or ginger cookies (see tip box, opposite).

Mix powdered sugar and water in small bowl until of a smooth consistency. Divide frosting among several bowls and add food coloring as desired. Use frosting to assemble pieces.

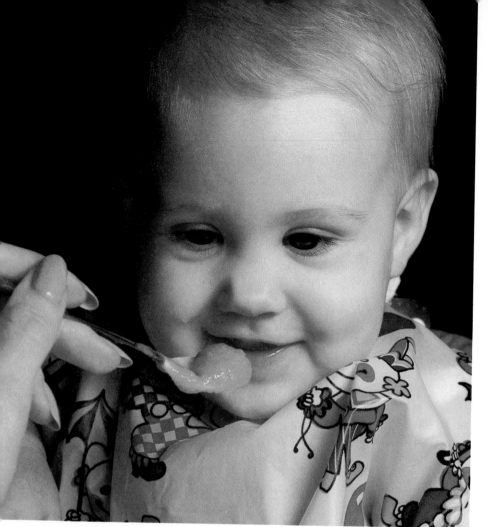

Baby Food

Microwaving vegetables and fruits for baby has the same advantages it does for adults. It's faster and needs less water than conventional cooking, so more nutrients are retained. The taste and color are fresh. Homemade baby food has no added salt, sugar or preservatives. Freeze it in single servings for quick defrosting in the microwave.

Formula and commercial baby food can also be warmed in the microwave oven. It takes just a few seconds.

How to Freeze & Defrost Homemade Baby Food

Freeze baby food in ¼-cup or ½-cup quantities in freezer bags or small jars. Or, place 2 tablespoons baby food in each section of ice cube tray. Freeze until solid; place cubes in freezer bag and seal. Label and freeze no longer than 6 months.

Defrost food in small bowl. Microwave as directed in chart, right, until warm, stirring and breaking apart with a fork after half the time. Test temperature before feeding baby.

Don't Overheat

Baby food and formula should be warmed, not heated. A safe temperature of 80° to 90°F. will feel slightly warm when a few drops of formula are sprinkled on the inner wrist.

Defrosting Baby Food Chart

Amount	Microwave Time at High
2 tablespoons (1 cube)	20 - 40 sec.
¼ cup (2 cubes)	45 - 60 sec.
½ cup (4 cubes)	1 - 2 min.

Cooking Vegetables for Homemade Baby Food Chart

Cook vegetables as directed. To purée cooked vegetables for baby food, follow directions, below.

Item	Amount	Cooked Yield	Microwave Time at High	Procedure
Sweet Potato (7 to 8 oz. each)	2	1½ cups	5 - 9 minutes	Pierce potatoes with fork. Place on paper towel. Rearrange after half the time. Peel and quarter.
Acorn Squash (1 lb.)	1	1 cup	5 - 7 minutes	Cut in half. Scoop out seeds and fibers. Wrap each half in plastic wrap. Rearrange after half the time. Scoop out pulp.
Carrots 1 lb.	6 medium	2 cups	7 - 9 minutes	Peel and slice ¼-in. thick. Place in 2-qt. casserole with ¼ cup water; cover. Stir every 2 minutes. Let stand, covered, about 5 minutes.
Frozen Loose-Pack Vegetables	1 cup	1 cup	4 - 6½ minutes	Place in 22-oz. casserole. Add 2 teaspoons water; cover. Stir 2 or 3 times.

Puréed Baby Food From Fresh Vegetables. Microwave vegetable as directed in chart, above. Place cooked vegetable in blender. Add ½ cup water. (Except acorn squash; use ¼ cup water.) Blend about 1 minute, or until puréed. If thinner consistency is desired, add up to an additional ¼ cup water.

Variation:
Puréed Baby Food From Frozen Vegetables. Microwave frozen vegetables as directed in chart, above. Place vegetables, cooking liquid and 3 to 5 tablespoons additional water in blender. Blend about 1 minute, or until puréed.

Applesauce. Peel and core four cooking apples. Chop finely. Place in 2-qt. casserole. Add ½ cup water; cover. Microwave at High 10 to 13 minutes, or until tender, stirring 1 or 2 times. Place in blender. Add 2 tablespoons sugar, if desired. Blend about 30 seconds, or until puréed. Makes about 2 cups.

Convenience Baby Food Chart

Item	Amount	Microwave Time at High: Room Temp.	Microwave Time at High: Refrigerated	Procedure
Baby Food Jars 3½ to 4¾ oz. or half of 7½ to 7¾ oz.	1 jar	15 - 30 sec.	30 - 40 sec.	Transfer food from jar to serving dish. Stir and check temperature after half the minimum time. Do not overheat. If necessary, continue microwaving. When microwaving two or more jars at a time, check temperature after minimum time and remove any food that is warm. Check temperature before feeding baby.
	2 jars	30 - 40 sec.	1 - 1¼ min.	
	3 jars	40 - 60 sec.	1¼ - 1½ min.	
Baby Formula	4 oz.	15 - 20 sec.	25 - 40 sec.	Use dishwasher-safe plastic or glass bottles for baby formula. Do not use bottles with plastic liners. The liners can melt in the microwave oven. Microwave, without cap and nipple, until warm. To test temperature, attach nipple and cap; shake bottle to distribute heat. Sprinkle few drops on inner wrist.
	6 oz.	20 - 30 sec.	30 - 45 sec.	
	8 oz.	30 sec.	45 - 60 sec.	

Snacks by Kids

Microwaving is a good way for children to learn to cook. It's safe because the oven doesn't get hot. In the excitement of sampling their results, children can forget to turn off a conventional oven or surface burner; the microwave oven turns off automatically, so less adult supervision is needed.

The speed and simplicity of microwave cooking appeal to children, who like to make uncomplicated foods which are done fast; otherwise they may become discouraged or lose interest. These nutritious snacks are so easy the children can cook and clean up themselves.

Hamburger. Place one ¼-lb. hamburger patty on microwave roasting rack. Cover with wax paper. Microwave at High 1 minute. Turn over; cover. Microwave 30 seconds to 1½ minutes, or until meat is no longer pink. Let stand 1 to 2 minutes.

For two patties, microwave first side 1½ minutes; turn. Microwave second side 1 to 2½ minutes.

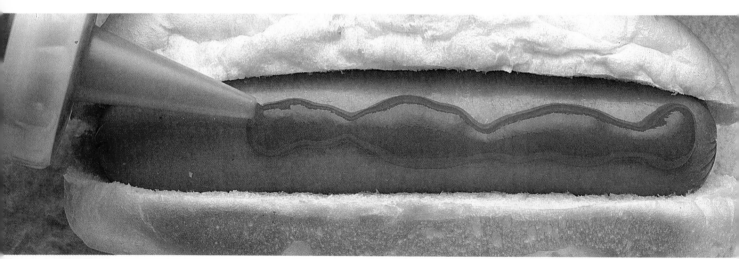

Hot Dog. Place one or two hot dogs in bun. Wrap each in paper towel. Microwave one at High 30 to 45 seconds, or two 45 seconds to 1¼ minutes, or until buns are warm to the touch, rearranging and rotating after half the time.

Pizza Crackers

4 saltine crackers
  Bottled pizza sauce
1 slice (¾ oz.) mozzarella
  cheese, quartered
4 thin slices pepperoni,
  optional

Serves 1

Spread crackers with pizza
sauce. Top each with a cheese
quarter and a slice of
pepperoni. Place on paper
plate. Microwave at 50%
(Medium) 30 to 60 seconds, or
until cheese melts, rotating plate
after 30 seconds.

Mini S'More Snacks

2 Graham Cracker Cookies,
  page 120, or 2 graham
  cracker squares
1 square of a milk chocolate
  candy bar (1.45 oz.), or
  6 chocolate chips
3 miniature marshmallows

Serves 1

Prepare Graham Cracker
Cookies as directed. Place one
cookie or cracker on paper
napkin or paper plate. Top with
chocolate square or chips and
marshmallows. Microwave at
High 15 to 30 seconds, or until
marshmallows just start to puff.
Top with second cookie.

Easy Fruit & Gelatin

1 can (17 oz.) fruit cocktail,
  packed in its own juice
⅓ cup water
1 box (3 oz.) fruit-flavored
  gelatin
1 cup cold water

Serves 4

In 1½-qt. casserole combine
fruit and juice with ⅓ cup water.
Microwave at High 4 to 7
minutes, or until boiling, stirring
after half the time. Mix in
gelatin, stirring until dissolved.
Stir in 1 cup cold water. Chill
until set.

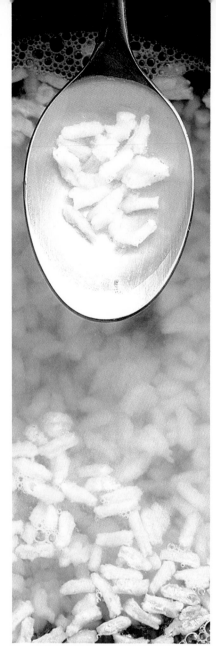

Cheese & Vegetables

½ cup frozen loose-pack
    vegetables
1 slice (¾ oz.) pasteurized
    process cheese

Serves 1

Place vegetables in 12-oz. bowl;
cover. Microwave at High 1 to 2
minutes, or until hot. Place
cheese on top of vegetables;
cover. Let stand 1 to 2 minutes,
or until cheese melts.

Chicken & Rice Soup

1 cup hot water
1 teaspoon instant chicken
    bouillon granules
2 tablespoons uncooked
    instant rice

Serves 1

In 2-cup measure or 15-oz. bowl
combine water and bouillon
granules. Microwave at High 1
to 2½ minutes, or until boiling.
Stir in rice. Cover with plastic
wrap and let stand 3 minutes,
or until rice is tender.

Vegetable-Beef Soup

1 cup hot water
½ cup frozen loose-pack mixed
    vegetables
1 teaspoon instant beef
    bouillon granules

Serves 1

In 2-cup measure or 15-oz.
bowl combine water, vegetables
and bouillon granules. Microwave at High 1½ to 3 minutes,
or until heated, stirring after half
the time to dissolve bouillon.

Mashed Potato

1 medium baking potato
1 tablespoon water
1 tablespoon butter or
 margarine
 Dash salt
 Dash pepper

Serves 1

Peel potato with vegetable peeler. Cut into ¾-in. cubes. Place in 15-oz. individual casserole or bowl. Sprinkle with water; cover. Microwave at High 2½ to 4 minutes, or until fork tender, stirring after half the time.

Add butter, salt and pepper to potato cubes; mash with fork.

Potato Salad ▶

1 medium baking potato
1 tablespoon water
2 tablespoons mayonnaise or
 salad dressing
1 tablespoon chopped celery
¼ teaspoon prepared mustard
⅛ teaspoon salt
 Dash onion powder
 Dash pepper

Serves 1

How to Microwave Potato Salad

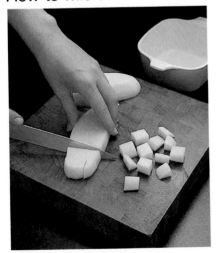

Peel potato with vegetable peeler. Cut into ¾-in. cubes. Place in 15-oz. individual casserole. Sprinkle with water.

Cover. Microwave at High 2½ to 4 minutes, or until fork tender, stirring after half the time.

Mix mayonnaise, celery, mustard, salt, onion powder and pepper in small custard cup. Spoon over potatoes, tossing to coat. For cold potato salad, refrigerate at least 30 minutes.

131

Dough Art

The microwave oven dries baker's clay in minutes rather than the hour or two needed conventionally. Use this inedible dough to make baskets, picture frames, ornaments, candle holders, necklace pendants or to sculpt small figures.

The dough can be applied to microwave oven-safe objects, such as clay pots or glass jars. To test dish safety, place in oven. Place ½ to 1 cup water in glass measure. Set on or next to dish. Microwave at High 1 to 2 minutes. If dish remains cool, it is microwave-safe. Before shaping dough over glass bottles, jars or bowls, check the glass carefully for flaws. Do not use imperfect glass, as heat and steam from the dough could cause it to break.

Always elevate objects on a microwave roasting rack. The dough adheres to glass and clay, so no glue is needed. If you plan to remove the shaped object from the glass after microwaving, first spray the glass with a non-stick vegetable cooking spray. Allow items shaped over glass to cool in the oven; rapid temperature changes can cause the glass to break.

Useful tools for dough art are a rolling pin; a ruler; cookie cutters, pastry cutter, drinking glass with floured rim, or a small knife for cutting out objects; a drinking straw for making holes to hang ornaments; flat wooden sticks for sculpting or engraving designs; wooden picks for interior support of arms, legs or neck of sculptured figures; garlic press to produce textures like hair or fur; and a paintbrush to moisten pieces for joining. After thorough drying, paint your work with acrylic or enamel colors or finish with a sealer to prevent brittleness.

◀ Dough Art

3 cups all-purpose flour
¾ cup salt
¾ teaspoon powdered alum

Food coloring, optional
1¼ cups water

In large bowl combine flour, salt and alum. If colored dough is desired, add food coloring to water. Mix water into flour. Shape dough into ball. Knead dough on lightly floured surface about 5 minutes, or until dough is smooth. Store in plastic bag.

If dough becomes too stiff, sprinkle lightly with water while kneading. If dough is too moist, knead in additional flour to achieve desired consistency. Most dough shapes are microwaved on microwave roasting rack or microwave baking sheet sprayed with non-stick vegetable cooking spray. Microwave at 30% (Medium-Low) at 2-minute intervals.

Microwave dough drying is *not* a complete drying process. Small areas of most objects may remain moist but firm to the touch. Allow all microwave-dried pieces to air-dry for at least 24 hours before finishing. All dried objects require finishing to prevent brittleness or breakage. Paint both sides of exposed areas with acrylic sealer, shellac, varnish or lacquer.

How to Microwave Baskets

Prepare dough as directed, page 133. Select glass bowl the size and shape desired for basket. Dough is shaped over outside of bowl. Spray outside of bowl with non-stick vegetable cooking spray. Place bowl upside down.

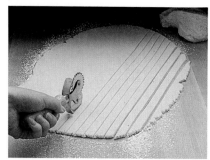

Roll dough on lightly floured surface to ¼-in. thickness. Using pastry wheel or knife, cut ½-in. wide strips long enough to go across side, bottom and other side of bowl with 1-in. overhang on each side.

Weave bottom by starting in center and laying parallel strips across bottom. Pull back every other strip to center and place another strip at right angles. Lift alternate strips and place another strip at right angles. Continue with additional strips until bottom is woven.

Cut ½-in. wide strips long enough to go around bowl. Weave in and out of strips on bowl until sides are completed. Join ends of strips by moisten-ing with small amount of water. (A paintbrush works well.) Trim strips even with top of bowl.

Form rope long enough to go around top of basket by rolling two equal pieces of dough between hands. Lay pieces side by side and twist one over the other, starting at center. Moisten top basket edge with water and press rope onto wo-ven pieces. Moisten ends to join.

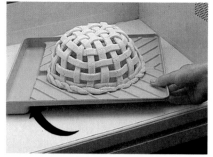

Microwave one basket at a time at 30% (Medium-Low) 4 minutes, rotating 2 or 3 times. Check; rotate if basket is not dry. Continue to microwave at 2-minute intervals, checking and rotating after each minute. Cool in oven. Remove from bowl and finish as directed, page 133.

How to Microwave Cookie Cut-Outs

Prepare dough as directed, page 133. Spray microwave baking sheet with non-stick vegetable cooking spray.

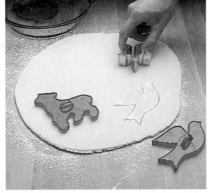

Roll dough on lightly floured surface to ¼-in. thickness. Dip edges of cutters in vegetable oil. Cut desired shapes.

Arrange four pieces at a time on prepared baking sheet. Cut-outs can be appliqued with small designs, if desired.

Shape designs for applique out of very small pieces of dough. Moisten area on cut-out to be decorated. Place applique on wet area, as directed, page 137.

Punch small hole at top of cut-out with wooden pick or drinking straw if object is to be hung. Microwave pieces at 30% (Medium-Low) 2 minutes.

Check; rotate if pieces are not dry. Continue microwaving at 2-minute intervals, checking and rotating after each minute. Cool and finish, as directed, page 133.

How to Microwave Picture Frames

Prepare dough as directed, page 133. Spray microwave baking sheet with non-stick vegetable cooking spray. Roll dough on lightly floured surface to ¼-in. thickness.

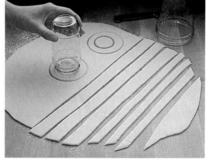

Use pastry wheel or knife to cut ½- to 1-in. wide strips long enough to form 3 × 5- or 5 × 7-in. rectangles. Cut circles with a jar, using a smaller jar to cut out center.

Assemble frame on prepared baking sheet. Wet cut edges with water and press together gently. Applique with cut-out designs, if desired.

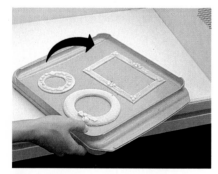

Microwave at 30% (Medium-Low) 2 minutes. Check; rotate if pieces are not dry. Microwave at 2-minute intervals, checking and rotating after each minute.

Cool and finish as directed, page 133. Cut cardboard to fit back and cover with fabric. Glue cardboard onto three edges of frame back.

Leave one edge of frame open to insert picture. Attach picture hanger, paper clip or easel backing.

How to Microwave Appliques for Clay Pots

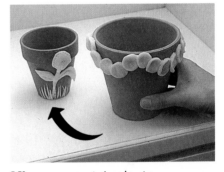

Prepare dough as directed, page 133. Cut or shape desired designs. Wet one side of cut-out designs and area on pot where designs are to be applied.

Press designs onto dampened surface. Place pot directly on oven floor. Microwave at 30% (Medium-Low) 2 minutes; check. Rotate if piece is not dry.

Microwave at 1-minute intervals, checking and rotating after each minute. Cool in oven. Finish as directed, page 133.

How to Microwave Decorated Jars

Prepare dough as directed, page 133. Roll dough on lightly floured surface to ¼-in. thickness. Press dough over jar until it adheres.

Applique as desired. Place in oven upside down on roasting rack. Microwave at 30% (Medium-Low) 2 minutes; check. Rotate if piece is not dry.

Microwave at 1-minute intervals, checking and rotating after each minute. Cool in oven. Finish as directed, page 133.

Food Tips

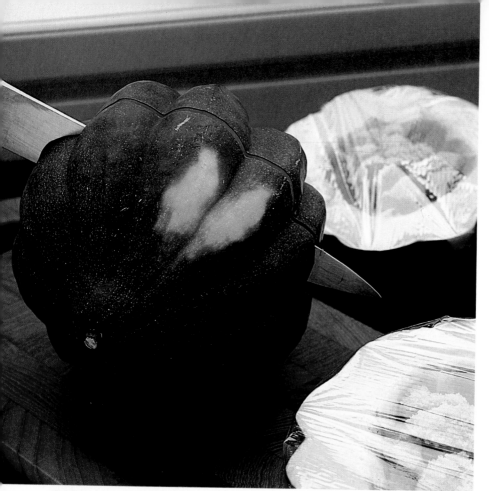

Soften Acorn Squash. Soften acorn squash to ease cutting. Microwave 1-lb. squash at High 1½ minutes, or until just warm to the touch. Halve and remove seeds. Place butter and brown sugar in cavity. Add nuts, if desired. Cover each half with plastic wrap. Microwave at High 6 to 10 minutes, or until tender.

Hard-Cook Eggs. To hard-cook eggs for chopping and adding to salads or casseroles, crack one egg into small, lightly greased bowl or custard cup. Prick yolk with wooden pick. Cover with plastic wrap. Microwave at 50% (Medium) 1¾ to 2 minutes, or until white is set and yolk is almost set. Let stand, covered, 1 minute to complete cooking.

Discover some of the microwave shortcuts and simple techniques you can use to make cooking easier. Soften an underripe avocado when there isn't time to let nature do it, or ease opening of fresh clams and oysters. Make your own yogurt, sweetened condensed milk, seasoned croutons, even dog biscuits. Add a pretty top crust to a microwaved pie, or speed conventional cooking by using the microwave to scald milk or rehydrate dried beans.

Soften Avocados. Use your microwave to soften underripe avocados, then use them in your favorite recipe. Microwave avocados at High 1 minute. Cool completely before slicing or mashing.

Warm Chow Mein Noodles. Before serving, place about 1 cup noodles at a time on serving plate. Microwave at High 1 to 1½ minutes, or until bottom center of plate is warm to the touch.

Drier Baked Potatoes. For drier skins on microwave baked potatoes, stand pierced potatoes on end in muffin cups.

Bacon-Basted Meats & Poultry. When microwaving roasts or whole poultry with very little natural fat cover, place strips of bacon over top of meat and secure with wooden picks. The bacon shields meat, attracts energy evenly and allows some browning while basting and flavoring the meat.

Warm Brandy. Place 2 ounces of brandy in snifter. Microwave at High 15 seconds to warm.

Rehydrate Dried Beans. Dried beans don't need to be soaked in water overnight. Place 1 lb. dried beans with 8 cups water in 5-qt. casserole; cover tightly. Microwave at High 8 to 10 minutes, or until boiling. Let stand, covered, 1 hour. Continue as directed in your favorite recipe.

Easy Tea. Heat water for brewing tea right in the teapot. Be sure teapot does not have any metal parts. Measure about 4 cups water into teapot; cover. Microwave at High 8 to 10 minutes, or until boiling. Add tea.

Two-Crust Pies. To give a microwaved one-crust pie a two-crust appearance, prepare a lattice top as directed, below, or prepare pastry cut-outs.

To make cut-outs, roll excess dough to ⅛-in. thickness and cut with cookie cutters. Or, cut out one 6- to 7-in. circle and prick with fork to mark six wedges.

Transfer pieces to wax paper, arranging pieces in ring.

Sprinkle with ground cinnamon and sugar. Microwave at High 2 to 4 minutes, or until dry and puffy, rotating after each minute. Place cut-outs on top of prepared pie.

How to Microwave Lattice Top

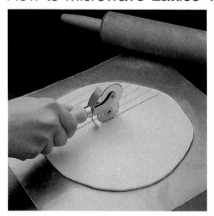

Roll excess pastry into 8-in. circle on wax paper. Cut into ten or twelve ½-in. wide strips.

Weave strips to form lattice on wax paper. Microwave at High 2 to 4 minutes, or until dry and puffy, rotating after each minute.

Remove lattice top from wax paper while warm. Place on top of the prepared pie.

Yogurt ▶

2½ cups non-fat dry milk
    powder
3½ cups water
 ⅓ cup plain yogurt

Makes 4 cups

Place dry milk in 2-qt. casserole or bowl. Slowly stir in water until dry milk dissolves. Microwave at High 8 to 12 minutes, or until temperature reaches 190°F., stirring 1 or 2 times. Let mixture cool to 115°F. Stir small amount of hot mixture into yogurt. Return to milk, stirring constantly. Cover with plastic wrap.

Insert microwave thermometer through plastic so it rests in center of milk mixture. If using 2-qt. casserole, thermometer will not stand up in center. Place thermometer in center periodically and check temperature. Reduce power to 30% (Medium-Low). When temperature falls below 115°F., microwave 30 seconds to 3½ minutes, or until temperature reaches 115°F.

Allow mixture to stand in oven undisturbed 3 to 4 hours, checking temperature every 30 minutes. When temperature falls below 110°F., microwave at 30% (Medium-Low) 30 to 60 seconds, or until temperature reaches 115°F. Mixture will appear set. Transfer to refrigerator to chill. Store in refrigerator no longer than 2 weeks.

Flavor Variations:

Stir one of the following into 1 cup yogurt:
· 2 tablespoons honey
· 2 teaspoons sugar and ½ teaspoon vanilla
· 2 teaspoons fresh lemon juice and 1 tablespoon sugar

Sweetened Condensed Milk

1½ cups non-fat dry milk
    powder
 ½ cup water
 ⅔ cup sugar
 1 teaspoon vanilla

Makes 1⅓ cups

In 4-cup measure mix dry milk and water until smooth. Stir in remaining ingredients. Microwave at High 30 seconds to 1½ minutes, or until heated but not boiling, stirring every 30 seconds. Substitute for one can (14 oz.) sweetened condensed milk.

Microwave & Save

It saves money to microwave your own sweetened condensed milk or yogurt. There's no need to purchase a special yogurt maker.

Scald Milk. Place ½ cup milk in 1-cup measure. Microwave at High 1 to 1½ minutes, or until thin film forms over top of milk and tiny bubbles form at edge of cup (about 175°F.).

For 1 cup milk, place in 2-cup measure; microwave at High 2 to 2¾ minutes.

▲ **Garlic Bread.** Place 2 tablespoons butter or margarine and ⅛ teaspoon garlic powder in small bowl. Microwave at High 30 to 45 seconds, or until butter melts. Add ⅛ teaspoon paprika to butter. Quarter three slices of bread. Brush garlic butter on pieces. Arrange bread, buttered side up, on microwave roasting rack. Microwave at High 3 to 4 minutes, or until dry and firm to the touch, checking after each minute. Cool on wire rack until crisp. Makes 12 pieces.

◄ **Warm Breads & Rolls in Basket.** Line nonmetallic basket with cloth napkin. Place bread or rolls in basket. Cover with napkin. To warm, microwave six rolls at High 15 seconds; ten rolls for 30 seconds; or one loaf (8 oz.) French bread for 30 seconds.

Croutons. Prepare croutons to use in salads or to top casseroles. Cut enough white, wheat, rye or other bread into ½-in. cubes to measure 4 cups. Spread cubes in 12 × 8-in. baking dish. Microwave at High 4 to 5 minutes, or until dry to the touch, stirring every 2 minutes. Let stand until cool.

Variations:

Herb-Seasoned Croutons:
Microwave 1 tablespoon butter or margarine at High 30 to 45 seconds, or until melted. Stir in 1 teaspoon dried parsley flakes, ½ teaspoon poultry seasoning, and ⅛ teaspoon salt. Toss cubed bread in seasoned butter. Microwave as directed.

Italian-Seasoned Croutons:
Microwave 1 tablespoon butter or margarine at High 30 to 45 seconds, or until melted. Mix in 1 tablespoon grated Parmesan or Romano cheese, 1 teaspoon dried parsley flakes, ⅛ teaspoon salt, and ⅛ teaspoon garlic powder. Toss cubed bread in seasoned butter. Microwave as directed.

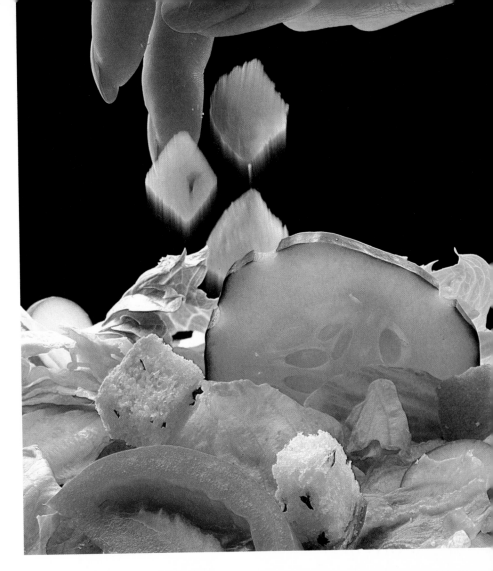

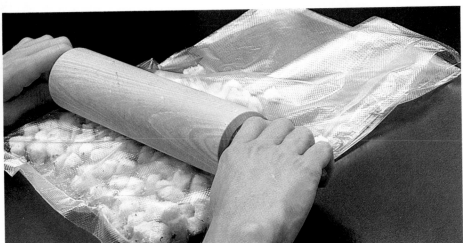

Bread Crumbs. Prepare bread crumbs to use for coating, toppings or as an ingredient in recipes. Microwave Croutons as directed, above. After cooling, crush in blender or place cubes in plastic bag and crush with rolling pin.

Variation:
Seasoned Bread Crumbs: Prepare Herb-Seasoned or Italian-Seasoned Croutons as directed, above. Crush.

Re-crisp Snack Foods. Stale snack foods such as potato chips, pretzels or popcorn can be re-crisped. Place 2 to 3 cups in small napkin-lined bowl or nonmetallic basket. Microwave, uncovered, at High 15 to 60 seconds, or until food is warm to the touch. Cool.

◀ **Elevating to Aid Cooking.** If any area in breads and quiches remains uncooked after recommended cooking time, elevate dish on inverted saucer and continue microwaving at 1-minute intervals. This will expose more of the uncooked area to microwave energy and aids in cooking.

Cakes and quick breads may have uncooked batter on the bottom center. Microwave until wooden pick inserted in center comes out clean.

Custard pies and quiches may sometimes have uncooked area on the top center. Microwave until knife inserted in center comes out clean.

How to Open Fresh Oysters & Clams

Clean oysters or clams. Soak in cold water at least 3 hours. Arrange six oysters at a time in 9-in. round cake dish or 2-qt. casserole. Cover with plastic wrap or lid.

Microwave at High 45 seconds, or until shells have just opened. Remove all opened shells and continue microwaving any unopened oysters, checking every 15 seconds.

Insert knife between shells near hinge and open. Use knife to cut muscle away from shell. To cook oysters or clams, microwave another 30 to 60 seconds, or until firm.

Drain Ground Beef. Microwave and drain ground beef at the same time. Crumble 1 lb. ground beef into dishwasher-safe plastic colander with no metal parts. Place colander in 2-qt. casserole or deep bowl. Microwave at High 4 to 6 minutes, or until meat is no longer pink, stirring with fork to break apart every 2 minutes.

Frozen Vegetable Pouches. If possible, flex pouch to break apart vegetables. Cut a large "X" in one side of pouch. Place 9- or 10-oz. pouch, cut side down, in serving dish. Microwave at High 5 to 8 minutes, or until heated. Lift opposite corners of pouch to protect your hands from steam as vegetable is released into dish. Stir.

Frozen Vegetables in Box. To defrost a 10-oz. package of frozen vegetables for use in a recipe, remove paper wrapping; place box on oven floor. Microwave at High 4 minutes, or until box is warm to the touch, turning after half the time. Let stand to complete defrosting. Drain. Add to recipe.

Cooking bags provide an easy clean-up method for roasting. When using cooking bags, tie loosely with string or rubber band to allow steam to escape. Do not use twist ties.

Leftover Rice. Freeze leftover rice in 1- or 2-cup quantities. Store no longer than 6 months. To defrost, place rice in casserole indicated in chart, below; cover. Microwave at High as directed, until hot, breaking apart and stirring once.

Amt.	Casserole Size	Microwave Time
1 cup	15-oz.	2 - 3 min.
2 cups	1-qt.	4 - 8 min.

Using Foil in the Microwave

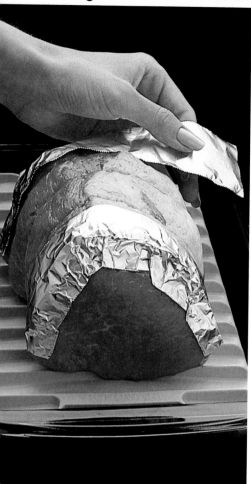

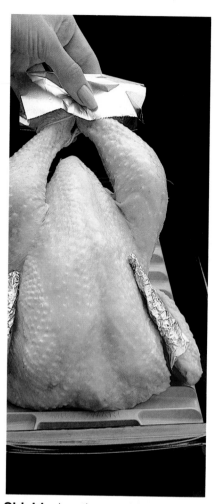

Use foil to shield and protect protruding angles and edges of roasts that may overcook because they are exposed to more microwave energy.

Shield wing tips and leg ends of chicken to prevent over-cooking during defrosting and microwaving.

Wrap baked potatoes and tent roasts with foil during standing time to hold in heat and complete cooking.

How to Defrost Half a Package of Frozen Food

Shield half of a frozen package, such as hot dogs, with enough foil to just loosely cover top and bottom. Foil reflects energy away from shielded area, allowing half the package to defrost, while the other half remains frozen.

Microwave at 50% (Medium) 1½ to 2½ minutes, or until unshielded side is cool and soft to the touch, but no longer icy. Remove defrosted hot dogs; return package to freezer.

Foil Tips

- Keep all foil at least 1 inch from oven walls.
- The amount of food should be three times the amount of foil (e.g. two-thirds of a roast should be exposed).
- Crinkles in foil can sometimes cause arcing. Smooth pieces to fit close to food.
- Frozen convenience foods in foil containers must be transferred to microwave-safe dish for defrosting or cooking. The exception is a TV dinner in a shallow container (¾-in.). Remove foil lid; microwave in container.

Dog Biscuits

1 cup whole wheat flour
½ cup all-purpose flour
¾ cup non-fat dry milk powder
½ cup quick-cooking rolled oats
¼ cup yellow cornmeal
1 teaspoon sugar
⅓ cup shortening
1 egg, slightly beaten
1 tablespoon instant chicken or
    beef bouillon granules
½ cup hot water

Makes 1½ dozen cut-outs
or 5½ dozen nuggets

Variation:
Cheese Dog Biscuits: Omit
bouillon granules. Add ¼ cup
canned grated American
cheese food to dry ingredients.
Continue as directed, below.

How to Microwave Dog Biscuits

Combine flours, milk powder, rolled oats, cornmeal and sugar in medium bowl. Cut in shortening until mixture resembles coarse crumbs.

Stir in egg. Stir instant bouillon granules into hot water until dissolved. Slowly pour into the flour mixture, stirring with a fork to moisten.

Form dough into ball and knead on floured board 5 minutes, or until smooth and elastic. Divide dough in half and roll out each ½ inch thick.

Make cut-outs with cookie cutter. Or, make nuggets by rolling dough into 1-in. diameter log; cut off ½-in. pieces.

Arrange six cut-out shapes or 24 nuggets on 10-in. plate. Microwave at 50% (Medium) 5 to 10 minutes, or until firm and dry to the touch.

Rotate plate every 2 minutes and turn shapes over after half the time. Cool on wire rack. Shapes will crisp as they cool.

Household Tips

The microwave oven is a cooking appliance, but you can also use it for household preparations other than cooking. Make your own liquid soap to extend a cake of expensive specialty soap. Create lip gloss from used lipsticks and petroleum jelly or leftover gloss. You can even make finger paints to amuse the children on a rainy day.

◀ Liquid Hand Soap

1 bar (3.5 oz.) soap with
    moisturizing cream
3 cups water

Makes 3 cups

How to Microwave Liquid Hand Soap

Shred bar of soap. Place in large bowl or 8-cup measure. Add water.

Microwave at High 5 to 6 minutes, or until soap is dissolved, stirring every 2 minutes.

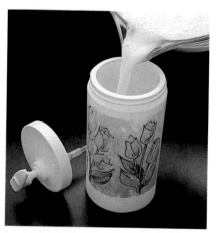

Let stand until cool. Mixture thickens as it cools. Fill soap dispensers.

Make New Lip Glosses

Combine light and dark lipstick pieces with equal amounts of petroleum jelly to create new lip gloss colors. If desired, add a drop of extract for flavor, such as vanilla, peppermint or lemon.

How to Microwave New Lip Gloss

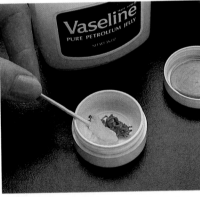

Save leftover stubs of lipstick and lip gloss. Scrape out lipstick from tube with flat wooden pick. Place in small hard plastic container.

Add enough leftover colored gloss or petroleum jelly to equal amount of lipstick.

Microwave at High 30 to 60 seconds, or until mixture can be stirred smooth, stirring every 15 seconds with wooden pick.

Warm Hand Lotion. Remove cap and place bottle in oven. Microwave at High 15 to 30 seconds, or until bottle feels warm to the touch, checking every 15 seconds. Closely watch hand lotions because they tend to heat quickly.

Warm Baby Oil. Remove cap and place 4-oz. glass or plastic bottle of baby oil in oven. Microwave at High 4 to 5 minutes, or until bottle is warm to the touch, checking after each minute.

◀ **Oshibori Towels.** Fold four dampened washcloths and place in non-metallic basket or shallow dish. Microwave at High 1 to 2 minutes, or until warm to the touch. Offer to guests before and after dining.

For scented washcloths, place lemon peel, studded with 4 whole cloves, in each washcloth. Microwave as directed. Remove lemon before using.

Warm Compress. Place one dampened washcloth in oven. Microwave at High 15 to 30 seconds, or until warm to the touch. Use as compress.

Easy Ironing of Linens. To make ironing of linens, tablecloths and napkins easy, sprinkle lightly with water. Place in 1-gallon plastic garbage bag. Twist end to close loosely. Microwave at High 1 minute, or until warm to the touch. Iron.

Hot Towels

Carefully check towels after microwaving. They may become very warm.

▲ **Oven Refresher.** For a quick oven refresher, place ½ cup water in 4-cup measure or bowl. Add one of the following fresheners. Microwave, uncovered, at High 1 to 2 minutes, or until boiling. Microwave 1 minute longer. Oven and kitchen will smell fresh and clean.

Fresheners:
• 2 slices fresh lemon, orange or lime
• 1 tablespoon lemon juice
• ¼ teaspoon ground cinnamon
• 8 whole cloves and 8 whole allspice
• 1 teaspoon baking soda

Easy Oven Cleaning. Place dampened dishcloth in oven. Microwave at High 15 to 30 seconds, or until warm but not hot. Wipe up spills or cooked-on foods in oven cavity with warm cloth.

Rainbow Finger Paints ▶

½ cup cornstarch
3 cups cold water, divided

Food coloring (red, yellow, green, blue, or one of the combinations below)

Place cornstarch in large bowl. Blend in 1 cup water. Add remaining water. Microwave at High 8 to 9 minutes, or until thickened, stirring every 2 minutes. Pour ½ cup thickened mixture into each of six small bowls. Add desired food coloring. Cool before using.

Color Chart

Desired Color	Number of Drops Food Coloring Required			
	Green	Yellow	Red	Blue
Blue-green	1	---	---	3
Orange	---	2	1	---
Purple	---	---	3	1
Violet	---	---	1	2
Yellow-green	1	12	---	---

Do Not Microwave Paraffin

Paraffin is transparent to microwave energy and will not melt. Follow manufacturer's directions on paraffin package for melting.

Microwave Don'ts

- Do not dry wet clothing in the microwave. Heat will cause clothes to shrink or ignite.

- Do not use metal twist ties in the microwave. Substitute string or rubber bands to close cooking bags.

- Do not dry wet papers in the microwave. Dyes in the paper may cause it to ignite.

- Do not cook eggs in the shell in the microwave. See page 140 for a safe way to microwave hard-cooked eggs. Do not reheat hard-cooked eggs in the microwave.

- Do not pop popcorn in brown paper bags, or in glass or plastic bowls in the microwave. Heat generated by the microwave may ignite paper, crack glass or melt plastic. Microwave popcorn in a microwave popcorn popper as directed on page 114.

- Do not microwave foods that require a crust, such as popovers, angel food cakes and puff pastries. The microwave oven cooks with moist heat, not dry heat, and may not produce desired results for these types of food.

- Do not can food in the microwave.

- Do not attempt to dry flowers, fruit, herbs, wood or gourds in the microwave.

- Do not use Melamine® or Centura® tableware in the microwave.

Index